Hiking Trails *of the* PACIFIC NORTHWEST

Hiking Trails *of the* PACIFIC NORTHWEST

OREGON and NORTHERN CALIFORNIA

WASHINGTON and SOUTHWESTERN BRITISH COLUMBIA

Photography by

BART SMITH

CRAIG ROMANO and **WILLIAM L. SULLIVAN**

Foreword by **DANIEL EVANS**

RIZZOLI
NEW YORK

New York · Paris · London · Milan

Contents

Foreword

DANIEL EVANS

Former Three-Time Governor of Washington and US Senator

The primitive Trapper Nelson packboard and open-fire cooking of my childhood hikes are now just fading memories. But I remember vividly one special hike of the past. In the 1950s, I led a Boy Scout Explorer Post. We spent a winter researching the first explorations of the Olympic Mountains and decided to retrace the US Army expedition of 1890 led by Lieutenant Joseph P. O'Neil.

In early September 1950, four of us began our journey at the trailhead on the Skokomish River. We soon left the trail and climbed the steep hillside to O'Neil Pass, descended to the Quinault River, climbed its most western ridge, and eventually crossed the Elwha River. We climbed the Elwha Snow Finger to Queets Basin, ascended Mount Olympus, and emerged from the mountains on the Hoh River Trail. It was a stunningly successful trip. We totaled 21,000 vertical feet of climbing and descending during seven sun-filled days. We watched hundreds of elk, enjoyed splendid views from the top of Mount Olympus, and created memories for a lifetime.

Today, weatherproof tents, featherweight stoves, down sleeping bags, and high-tech food options draw thousands of new visitors to our protected wilderness areas each year. We are in danger of loving our wilderness to death. The adage "Leave your campsite better than you found it" must be the goal of every visitor to our unique outdoor preserve.

Several generations of politically active citizens worked tirelessly to protect our precious lands. They presented ambitious proposals to Congress, culminating in the Washington State Wilderness Act of 1984. The bipartisan delegation gathered in Congressman Tom Foley's office, went in to two marathon private sessions (to the consternation of our staffs), and produced a one-million-acre addition to wilderness in Washington State. It was a memorable feat of lawmaking by the congressmen.

We now live in an information-cluttered age. Too often we are guilty of huddling behind our iPhones browsing websites and sending text messages, sometimes to friends in the same room. We are missing the experience of the natural world we have inherited and will hopefully pass on to future generations.

I remember with fondness that, when I was governor, our family planned multiday hikes in the Olympic Mountains. It was an opportunity for me to escape for a brief moment the formality and intensity of public office. Our youngest son, Bruce, pleaded to join us, but seemed too young. Finally, he reached eight years of age and I told him that he could join the trip, but would have to carry his own pack and keep up on the trail. He promised, and proved to be a strong hiker and an eager observer of wildlife. One morning, in the middle of the Olympics, the two of us sat for a rest in a gorgeous green meadow tattooed

Mount Olympus through spruce trees from the High Divide above Seven Lakes Basin, Olympic National Park, Washington

with an explosion of wildflowers. Our conversation quieted, and the hum of honeybees filled the air while a young bear calmly grazed a short distance away. Never had I felt closer to my son. There were no visible signs of civilization, and I thought this must be what it was like before humans touched the earth.

I often hear citizen volunteers—who labored for years to create wilderness protection—cheer when an avalanche destroys an approach road or floods wash away a vital bridge. They proclaim that this creates a deeper wilderness. But it also narrows the number of enthusiastic protectors. We need to create a balance of protection and availability. We must build a new generation of devoted walkers, hikers, and climbers who experience the love of wilderness and will fight to protect it. Otherwise, we will end up with an aging and shrinking cohort of zealous advocates, increasingly unable to fend off the constant pressure for development. This could radically diminish wilderness protection.

It is never easy. The population of Washington State has more than tripled in my lifetime. Demands for development push hard against the protection of natural areas. Citizen activists are the front line of protection, and smart and devoted workers will be vital to saving our wilderness experience.

Enjoy this splendid book. Trip destinations and good advice will help make your adventure a happy and successful one. Hike gently and slowly on the land. Stop regularly to sit back and listen to the voices. Hear the sharp whistle of a marmot, the thin cry of an eagle, and the soft growl of a bear. Enjoy the brief, peaceful moments of solitude and the joy of companionship with those who share your wilderness experience.

Hoh River Trail, Olympic
National Park, Washington

OREGON *and* NORTHERN CALIFORNIA

William L. Sullivan

The Pacific Northwest—once known as the Oregon Country—has always been a land of trails. Excavations in the caves of Eastern Oregon keep turning up ancient sandals—hiking shoes woven from sagebrush bark. DNA recovered from those caves suggests that the first people in North America arrived more than 14,000 years ago from Siberia, apparently by walking. Later pioneers on the Oregon Trail brought wagons, but most people walked beside them on that 2,000-mile trek.

This history of hiking lingers in the Oregon Country as a restless urge to hit the trail. Oregonians are not gladly caged inside office buildings or traffic jams. When the rains lift, people find themselves looking out the window, longing for the freedom of the map's wide, open spaces. In Oregon, where the number one religious affiliation is "none of the above," it is not uncommon to spend weekends in the Church of the Great Outdoors, recharging one's spirit by hiking through a cathedral grove of ancient firs or backpacking in a lonely desert canyon beneath the stars.

Even the cities in Oregon have hiking trails—not merely paved park paths, but real forest trails. Portland's Forest Park is the largest urban natural area in the country. From the midst of downtown's skyscrapers, you can ride the MAX Light Rail 2 miles into a tunnel, take an elevator 400 feet up to ground level, and set out on the Wildwood Trail, a 30-mile path through forested hills with hardly a glimpse of the surrounding city. Eugene's Ridgeline Trail similarly traces a forested crest around that town. Bend's Deschutes River Trail pursues the river through a rimrock canyon. Volunteers in Corvallis have pioneered a 100-mile Corvallis-to-the Sea Trail that crosses the Coast Range to the beach. In the Medford area, work continues on a 40-mile path along ridges from Jacksonville to Ashland—named the Jack-Ash Trail, of course. For the best scenery, however, you need to get out of town.

COLUMBIA RIVER GORGE

For Portlanders, the escape of first choice is the Columbia River Gorge. Here the mile-wide Columbia River squeezes through the Cascade Range in a 4,000-foot-deep chasm lined with waterfalls. The most popular trail in Oregon climbs beside the tallest of these cascades—the two-tiered, 620-foot Multnomah Falls. The parking lot for this waterfall has become so crowded that a sign beside the I-84 freeway is often lit: "Exit Closed; Lot Full." Undeterred, Portlanders ride shuttle buses to the trail.

The Oregon side of the gorge was developed for recreation early, with parks connected in 1916 by a scenic, twisting pleasure drive—now the Historic Columbia River Highway State Trail. Some of the same stoneworkers who built that road also chiseled out the Eagle Creek Trail. The rock walls of the creek's

PREVIOUS SPREAD: View from Painted Hills Overlook Trail, Painted Hills Unit, John Day Fossil Beds National Monument, Oregon

Multnomah Falls, Columbia River Gorge, Oregon

canyon are so steep that the crews sometimes notched ledges into the cliffs for the tread. It's just more than 2 miles to Punchbowl Falls, which plunges 30 feet into a mossy rock bowl. Another 4 miles upstream, the trail builders blasted a tunnel through the cliff behind the 200-foot plume of Tunnel Falls.

In 2017, a 15-year-old hiker trying to impress his friends with illegal fireworks accidentally ignited the Eagle Creek Fire in this canyon. As 50,000 acres burned, the skies of Portland darkened. When the Eagle Creek Trail reopened three years later, hikers were relieved to discover that most trees had survived and the understory was once again green.

Trail development on the Washington side of the Columbia Gorge began more slowly. In 1915, a man named Henry Biddle bought Beacon Rock, an 848-foot basalt monolith across the river from Multnomah Falls. He arduously constructed a hiking trail to the top, incorporating 47 switchbacks and dozens of railed catwalk bridges. Biddle wanted to donate the rock and its vertiginous trail as a state park. At first Washington refused because it had no state park system. But that decision quickly changed when *Oregon* offered to accept.

The eastern end of the gorge is a drier place, in the rain shadow of the Cascade Range. In April and May, when clouds cover western skies, hikers head east to climb sunny trails amid spring wildflowers.

Columbia River from Pacific Crest Trail, Columbia Wilderness, Oregon

OPPOSITE: Eagle Creek above Punchbowl Falls, Columbia Wilderness, Oregon

On Dog Mountain, atop Coyote Wall, and at The Nature Conservancy's Tom McCall Preserve, the slopes are ablaze with balsamroot, a native sunflower. Many of the viewpoint hikes require staggering elevation gains: 2,800 feet to Dog Mountain, 4,000 feet from Multnomah Falls to Larch Mountain, and fully 4,800 feet from Starvation Creek Falls to Mount Defiance.

Surprisingly, one of the best overlooked hikes in the Columbia Gorge is on the Pacific Crest Trail (PCT). At Cascade Locks, the PCT crosses the Columbia River on the Bridge of the Gods, a lacy 1926 steel span named for a Native American legend. Oregon author Cheryl Strayed ended her best-selling memoir, *Wild: From Lost to Found on the Pacific Crest Trail*, at this bridge. If you hike the PCT 2.4 miles south from the bridge, you'll find Dry Creek Falls, a very wet 50-foot waterfall that sprays out of a slot in a 300-foot cliff. Keep going, and you'll gain nearly 4,000 feet of elevation in 5 miles to the forested Benson Plateau. And if you still keep going, you can follow the PCT another 25 miles to Mount Hood.

MOUNT HOOD

Oregon's tallest peak has long been both an obstacle and a magnet for trail builders. Pioneers on the Oregon Trail brought wagons across Eastern Oregon, but quailed at the thought of rafting them down the dangerous rapids of the Columbia River. Sam Barlow eyed Mount Hood and announced, "God never made a mountain without a way over it or under it, and I'm going to try." The route he blazed was so awful that none of the wagons made it through the first year. His group nearly starved before hiking onward to Oregon City. But Barlow went back, built a barely passable wagon road beside Mount Hood, and made a living by charging a steep toll. Today, the Pioneer Bridle Trail west of Government Camp follows part of the old Barlow Road's harrowing route.

Mount Hood is said to be the second-most-climbed snow peak in the world—after Japan's sacred Mount Fuji. In 1893, Portland's outdoor club, the Mazamas, held its organizational meeting atop the 11,240-foot summit, with 155 men and 38 women scaling the peak to elect the club's first president. Since then, Mount Hood has been climbed by a man with no legs, a woman in high heels, and a gibbon named Kandy. But the mountain claims a life every year or so, proof that this is a serious climb and not a hike.

Climbers typically set out from Timberline Lodge, which is where you can also start some of the mountain's best hikes. The lodge itself was built in the depths of the Great Depression as a federal make-work program, employing 7,250 artisans. By the time President Franklin Roosevelt dedicated the huge stone-and-timber building in 1937, it had become a grand expression of Pacific Northwest art. But who, during a depression, would book a room at a mile-high lodge on a barren timberline slope? In order to attract more visitors, planners added one of North America's first ski resorts, opening the Magic Mile chairlift in 1939. In summer, you can hike the Mountaineer Trail 1 mile up from Timberline to see the old chairlift's restored turnaround building, the scenic Silcox Hut.

In another attempt to lure visitors to Timberline in the 1930s, the Civilian Conservation Corps built the 40-mile Timberline Trail around the mountain. Crews constructed four small stone huts along the route, reasoning that backpackers could hike the loop in five days, but then would be tempted to stay at Timberline Lodge twice. This ruse still works, in part because the lodge truly is a romantic trailhead, with

Descending Mount Hood, Mount Hood Wilderness, Oregon

quaint rooms, a heated outdoor pool, and a pub overlooking a gigantic stone fireplace. On the Timberline Trail itself, three of the historic 10-foot-square shelters have survived: at McNeil Point, in Cairn Basin, and on Cooper Spur. Although the shelter at Paradise Park was crushed by a tree in 1994, the wildflower meadows there remain one of Mount Hood's most scenic destinations, a rewarding 6-mile hike west of Timberline Lodge.

The PCT merges with the Timberline Trail around Mount Hood's western shoulder. Visitors can hike a bit of both routes on the 7.3-mile loop to Ramona Falls, a 120-foot cascade that spills over stairstepped columnar basalt like white lace. But this otherwise easy hike highlights one of the hazards of hiking around the big volcano—a lack of bridges. As the climate warms, Mount Hood's glaciers are melting, launching glacial floods. After several hikers died at bridged crossings, the Forest Service realized it could limit crowds and its liability by removing the bridges altogether. Hikers are now warned to cross glacial outwash creeks at their own risk, preferably in the early morning before snowmelt turns them into raging torrents.

Want to reflect on the mountain without that kind of stress? Then hike the easy loops around Trillium Lake or Lost Lake for their picture-postcard views, mirroring the snowy peak. Want to see giant trees instead? Hike through the old-growth groves along the nearby Salmon River. Want to soak in a hot pool that's wilder than the one at Timberline? Hike 1.5 miles to Bagby Hot Springs, where cedar logs have been hollowed into tubs big enough for two. There you can choose your heat by uncorking near-boiling water from an adjacent trough or by dipping icy water from a creek-fed vat.

CENTRAL OREGON CASCADES

South of Mount Hood, the PCT passes a string of spectacular Cascade volcanoes from Mount Jefferson to the Three Sisters. Near the recreation boomtown of Bend, this central part of the state has become so popular that the Forest Service limits crowds by requiring hikers to buy advance permits for heavily used trails. All summer, backpackers in the Mount Jefferson, Mount Washington, and Three Sisters Wilderness Areas have to buy permits online, with the quantity available each day limited to the number of reasonable campsites.

The most hotly desired of these limited tickets wins you admission to wildflower meadows snuggled up so close to a mountain that crags seem to fill half the sky. The Shangri-La at Mount Jefferson, Oregon's second-tallest peak, is Jefferson Park. This square-mile basin of swimmable lakes and flower meadows can be reached by three different trails, each with its own attraction. From Breitenbush Lake in the north, the PCT climbs over Park Ridge on its way to Jefferson Park, adding extra elevation gain but offering the best views of Mount Jefferson. From the southwest, the Whitewater Trail is the easiest route to the park, although it traverses 4 miles of snags left by a 2017 wildfire. From the west, the South Breitenbush Trail is unburned, but longer and rockier.

The next peak to the south, Three Fingered Jack, is 2,656 feet shorter than Mount Jefferson, but rises like a wall above the wildflowers of Canyon Creek Meadows. Glaciers have carved this extinct volcano into a colorfully striped palisade with three summit fingers. The 4.5-mile loop to the meadow is easy enough for hikers with children, and it's so popular that you'll not only need a permit, but also be asked to hike the loop clockwise so you'll meet fewer people.

View of Three Sisters and Mount Washington from Pacific Crest Trail, Oregon

Mount Washington, the next volcano in the Cascade parade, presides over miles of jagged black lava rather than wildflower meadows. To see it, drive the twisty old highway to McKenzie Pass, and then hike the PCT 2.4 miles north across the lava to a higher pass with a close-up view of the mountain. To your left is Belknap Crater, a red cinder cone whose eruption 1,300 years ago blanketed 100 square miles with ash. After that blast, a lava flow from the crater's base poured 12 miles west to dam the McKenzie River.

The Three Sisters dominate Central Oregon's horizon like the world's largest triple-scoop sundae. If you score a permit for the Obsidian Trail, a 12-mile loop will take you through some of the yummiest terrain—wildflower meadows, lakelets, and waterfalls beside North and Middle Sisters. Equally delicious are the lakes and wildflowers of the Green Lakes Basin, on the opposite side of the sundae between South Sister and Broken Top.

Each of the Sisters is more than 10,000 feet tall, but only South Sister is still an active volcano. Red petroglyphs mark the end of a 1,200-year-old lava flow on the mountain's south flank, where chunky basalt dammed Hell Creek to create Devils Lake. The rock art and demonic names suggest that native tribes recognized this as a place of violent power. South Sister is also the only major Central Oregon Cascade peak with a trail to its summit. Start in the predawn darkness at Devils Lake and be prepared to gain 4,900 feet of elevation if you plan to slog up the ash all the way to Teardrop Pool, a mostly frozen lake in the summit crater.

To skip the permit hassles, hike instead at Diamond Peak, Waldo Lake, or the lower, western peaks of the Old Cascades—or follow one of the area's many river trails. The 26.5-mile McKenzie River Trail follows that whitewater torrent from its source at Clear Lake, over roaring Sahalie Falls, and then underground. The entire McKenzie River disappears into a lava tube for 3 miles, emerging at the base of a dry waterfall in Tamolitch Pool, a chilly, stunningly turquoise lake also known as "Blue Pool."

SOUTHERN OREGON

Crater Lake is the state's only national park, but a surprisingly large percentage of Oregonians have never been there—or have only driven around the lake while entertaining out-of-state visitors. The problem is that automobiles were a trendy new rage in the years after the giant volcanic caldera achieved park status in 1902, so early rangers built a Rim Road rather than a Rim Trail. Today, only a few relatively short trails have views of the astonishingly deep blue lake, but it's definitely worth getting out of the car for these paths. The most popular, at Cleetwood Cove, is the only trail down to the lake itself. It's just 1.1 miles, but it's tougher than it first seems because you have to gain 700 feet of elevation back up to your car. Trails up Garfield Peak, The Watchman, and Mount Scott offer wider views and a friendlier downhill return route.

Where are Oregonians hiking, if not at Crater Lake? Actually, neighboring Diamond Lake is twice as popular with locals. Warmer, shallower, and more accessible, it's ringed with campgrounds and an 11.5-mile bike path. Out-of-state tourists also overlook popular, short hikes on the way to Crater Lake. If you're driving to the park from Roseburg, stop along the North Umpqua River to hike to Toketee Falls and a half dozen other hidden cascades, each less than a mile from trailheads beside the highway. If you're

Toketee Falls along North Umpqua River, Umpqua National Forest, Oregon driving to Crater Lake from Medford, stop for a walk to Takelma Gorge or Natural Bridge, where lava flows from Crater Lake's volcano have tortured the Upper Rogue River into chasms and tunnels.

South of Crater Lake, the PCT traverses the lake-dotted Sky Lakes Wilderness for 40 miles without once visiting a lake. How is this possible? The PCT was built in the 1960s as a bypass, intentionally routing long-distance hikers away from fragile lakeshores and scenic meadows. Forty years earlier, the old Oregon Skyline Trail had been built along the length of the state's Cascade Range with the opposite motive: to visit lakes and meadows where rangers could water and feed their horses. Much of that older route still exists under different names. South of Crater Lake, for example, you'll pass 40 lakes in 40 miles if you leave the PCT to explore the trails of the Seven Lakes Basin, the Blue Lake Basin, and the Sky Lakes Basin—all of them more beloved by locals than the viewless PCT.

The Siskiyou Mountains divide Oregon from California like a jagged picket fence. Where the PCT heads south into the Golden Bear State, the older, less-known Boundary Trail continues west along the range's crest to Oregon Caves National Monument. Here rangers lead hikers underground through vast vaults of limestone stalactites hailed by poet Joaquin Miller as the "great Marble Halls of Oregon."

The grandest of all Southern Oregon hikes, however, is the 40-mile Rogue River Trail through the Klamath Mountains toward the sea. Floating the green-pooled river along this route is so popular with kayakers and rafters that only 120 permits a day are issued from 90,000 applications. Backpackers have it much easier. Not only are the trail permits unlimited, but if you book ahead you can lighten your pack (and your wallet) by staying each night at lavish riverside lodges accessible only by boat or trail.

NORTHERN CALIFORNIA

Far Northern California tried to secede from the rest of the state in the early 1940s, hoping to join with Southern Oregon to form a new State of Jefferson. Lingering from that effort is a sense of disenfranchisement—and the Jefferson Public Radio station. To this day, trails in the area between Redding and the border seem to have fallen off the map for the crowds in San Francisco. While trailheads on the southern side of the Trinity Alps Wilderness are often packed with Priuses, trails on the "Jefferson" side are delightfully overlooked.

In addition to the Trinity Alps—a huge wilderness with peaks that really do resemble the Alps—this hidden corner of California includes hiking getaways in the Castle Crags, Russian, Marble Mountain, and Siskiyou Wilderness Areas. The best destinations here are the hundreds of mountain lakes in rocky bowls that were scooped out of the northern sides of summits in the Ice Age by now-vanished glaciers. Some lakes have no trail at all, but can be reached by cross-country scrambles through the sparsely forested subalpine terrain. Unlike trails in the High Cascades, which remain buried under snow until August, the trails here are usually snow-free by the end of June. The rock is arguably prettier too—polished white marble and speckled granite instead of black lava. Lakes are sandy bottomed instead of muddy, and warm enough by July for swimming. The drawback? Beginning on August 1, cattle are often allowed to graze, making late summer a season of cowbells, dust, and flies.

Rogue River Trail, Wild
Rogue Wilderness, Oregon

The PCT traverses five wilderness areas in far Northern California, but misses the greatest prize of all—Mount Shasta. The 14,162-foot volcano looms like a white ghost in the sky, twice the height of most nearby peaks. The local Wintu tribe held it taboo to venture above timberline, claiming that Shasta was the great white wigwam of a spirit whose cooking fire sometimes wafted sulfuric smoke from the summit. Those who smile at the Native American myth might note that a Rosicrucian author in 1931 claimed the mountain was inhabited by Lemurians, beings from the lost continent of Mu who hollowed out Mount Shasta with supersonic bells. Later, a Chicago paperhanger named Guy W. Ballard launched the I AM movement, based on his revelations at Mount Shasta from Saint Germain, a spiritual presence from the court of King Louis the 14th with a walnut-sized sense organ on his forehead.

Mount Shasta is so big and so isolated that it never ceases to inspire. Hikers who set out from timberline trailheads on the paved Everitt Memorial Highway are likely to see dream catchers on tree branches and stacked prayer stones by the path. The highest trailhead, at a huge parking lot where the highway ends, was built for a ski resort—despite the objections of the Wintu, who warned about their taboo. A later avalanche wiped out the resort's chairlifts and buildings, leaving only the parking lot.

For inspiration, it's hard to top the giant redwoods of the Northern California coast. The world's tallest living things, the trees here tower as high as 36-story buildings. Redwood National Park is the area's top tourist draw, but it's actually a fairly recent park of mostly cutover land. A *National Geographic* exposé in 1963 revealed that a grove with the tallest trees in the world was scheduled to be logged. Amid the resulting outrage, President Lyndon Johnson's wife, Lady Bird, championed the cause of preservation. In 1969, President Richard Nixon dedicated the park in a redwood grove named for the former first lady. The 1.4-mile loop trail here is still a good place to begin a visit, conveniently near Highway 101. But trees in the Lady Bird Johnson Grove are only 250 feet tall. The giant grove that sparked the furor is 6 miles inland, on a bend of Redwood Creek. Amazingly few people hike up the creekside trail 6.6 miles to the Tall Trees Grove, although no permit is required.

Truth be told, the most extensive stands of big redwoods are not in the national park at all, but rather in three adjacent state parks that were set aside in the 1920s. For a quick wow, stroll through the Stout Grove in Jedediah Smith Redwoods State Park, just inland from Crescent City. For a longer wow, consider trekking north along the ocean shore, following the Oregon Coast Trail (OCT).

NORTHERN OREGON COAST

Most people hike the OCT from north to south, from the Washington border at the Columbia River to the California redwoods. This direction makes sense because summer breezes often blow from the north—and because the northern part of the trail is more nearly complete. Of Oregon's 360 miles of coastline, only about 100 had been developed with trail tread in 2018, when the state legislature authorized completion of the route. Another 200 miles consisted of beaches. Oregon's beaches have all been public since 1913, when a cagey governor declared them state highways in order to save them for the public. Those long, sandy stretches were later transferred to the Oregon State Parks Department, and serve well enough as hiking trails, although walking in sand can be tiring. But what about the remaining 60 miles of the route, where

Jedediah Smith Redwoods
State Park, California

hikers have to walk the shoulder of busy Highway 101? It turns out that the public right-of-way along the highway is often quite wide, so volunteers are at work building tread through the woods on the ocean side of the highway's shoulder. Each year the OCT is more nearly complete.

Even if you don't tackle the entire OCT, you might hike the first few miles through Fort Stevens State Park. Seabirds cry and giant waves crash on the rock jetty at the Columbia River's mouth. On the beach are the rusting remains of the *Peter Iredale*, a four-masted ship that missed the river's entrance in 1906. Trails lead inland through the woods to Oregon's largest state campground (with nearly 500 campsites) and the visitable gun batteries of a fort that was shelled by a Japanese submarine in 1942.

A dozen miles south, hikers can follow the OCT along the rim of a 1,000-foot coastal cliff at Tillamook Head. The 7-mile hike through Ecola State Park from Seaside to Cannon Beach is just as panoramic as in 1806, when Captain William Clark hiked it in search of a beached whale. In the journals of the Lewis and Clark Expedition, he wrote, "I beheld the grandest and most pleasing prospects which my eyes ever surveyed."

Because Clark turned back at Cannon Beach, having bargained with natives for a share of the beached whale's blubber, he was unable to compare Tillamook Head with other spectacular coastal hikes farther south. On the other end of Cannon Beach, for example, a 12-mile section of the OCT skirts a hidden surfing beach at Smugglers Cove. Then the trail passes the churning chasm of Devils Cauldron and climbs to a breathtaking ocean view atop 1,600-foot Neahkahnie Mountain.

At Cape Lookout near Tillamook, a side trail of the OCT follows a basalt promontory that juts 2.4 miles straight out into the Pacific Ocean. Migrating whales detour around the cliffy tip, spouting below the trail. At Cascade Head near Lincoln City, hikers switchback up through butterfly meadows seemingly suspended above the sea. A waterfall pours directly into the ocean at a cove with so many sea lions that their barking can be heard a mile away.

Some of the most interesting coastal headland hikes visit lighthouses. At Yaquina Head near Newport, trails lead from the state's tallest lighthouse to an overlook on a hill and a beach of spherical black cobbles. At Heceta Head near Florence, the OCT climbs 1.3 miles through windswept woods to a lighthouse that still uses its original 1893 Fresnel lens. Weighing two tons, the lens aligns 640 prisms that were hand ground in Paris, sending a beam of light 20 miles out to sea. Beside the trail, an elegant white Queen Anne duplex once housed the two assistant lighthouse keepers. Now it's a bed-and-breakfast with spendy but spectacular rooms for hikers—and a resident ghost named Rue.

SOUTHERN OREGON COAST

There are no bluffs along the shore between Reedsport and Coos Bay, so beach sand blows inland, creating gigantic 300-foot dunes that swallow entire forests. Half of the 36-mile-long Oregon Dunes National Recreation Area is open to dune buggies, but hikers rule the rest. This is the place to find intact sand dollars on empty beaches, romp down rippled dunes, or set up a backpacking tent by a sand-rimmed lake. A favorite hike follows Tahkenitch Creek through the dunes to the sea. Maps here are unreliable, because storms every winter realign the creek, the dunes, and the trail.

Heceta Head Lighthouse
from Oregon Coast Trail,
Heceta Head Lighthouse State
Scenic Viewpoint, Oregon

At the mouth of Coos Bay, huge ocean waves smash onto tilted sandstone cliffs, sending spray a hundred feet in the air. Starfish roam the rocks of hidden coves. Elephant seals roar from offshore islands. Coos Bay timber baron Louis Simpson bought a mile of shoreline here as a Christmas surprise for his wife in 1906. Their oceanfront mansion burned in 1921, but the formal gardens and the stunning coastal trail remain as Shore Acres State Park. From there, you can hike 2 miles along the cliffs to Cape Arago. Return on an inland loop past the concrete bunker of a Coast Guard outpost where observers in World War II watched for Japanese attacks.

North of Brookings, Highway 101 threads through the cliffy coastal strip of Samuel H. Boardman State Scenic Corridor. But so does a 12.7-mile section of the OCT, and because the trail touches the highway every few miles, it's easy to hike the route in segments. You could also drive from one trailhead to the next, stopping to hike short paths out to viewpoints. On the 0.2-mile path from Arch Rock Picnic Area, you'll see an island with a sea-level hole. At Natural Bridges, waves have cut two tunnels through a cove's seawall. At Thomas Creek, the highway soars 345 feet above a seafront canyon on Oregon's tallest bridge. At Whaleshead Beach, there really is an island shaped like a whale. When the tide is right, waves spew up in a spouting horn from its head.

The redwoods on the Southern Oregon coast are not as big as those in California. On Wheeler Ridge, 10 miles inland from Brookings, a trail leads to an Oregon redwood grove with an interesting history. In 1942, the same Japanese submarine that had shelled Oregon's Fort Stevens returned to bomb the American mainland with a different weapon—a plane launched off a ramp on the submarine's deck. The pilot, Lieutenant Nobuo Fujita, successfully dropped a 500-pound incendiary bomb on Wheeler Ridge, intending to start a forest fire that would frighten the enemy. But redwoods are fireproof, so the bomb merely left a crater and a few charred trees.

The attack on Wheeler Ridge was quickly hushed up by the military. Forty years later, however, the Forest Service built a trail to the crater. For the opening ceremonies, they invited the Japanese pilot who had dropped the bomb. Retired Lieutenant Fujita had some misgivings about this invitation. Fearing that he might be put on trial as a war criminal, he brought his family's 400-year-old samurai sword. If worse came to worst, he planned to commit ritual suicide. But Fujita was welcomed as an ambassador of peace. He planted a redwood seedling in the crater. And then he donated his family's sword to the city of Brookings, where it hangs in the public library to this day.

All of Oregon's coastal trails are peaceful, but the trail on Wheeler Ridge—where a small redwood tree is now growing in a small crater—has a particularly strong message of peace.

WALLOWAS AND BLUES

Eastern Oregon—the vast arid landscape beyond The Dalles and Bend—is even more sparsely populated today than it was a century ago. Ghost towns dot the map, reminders of faded booms for gold, sheep, timber, and dryland farming. Today, the area's spectacular trails are providing a more permanent economic boost. Case in point: the Wallowa Mountains.

Whaleshead Beach, Samuel
H. Boardman State Scenic
Corridor, Oregon

Tucked into the remote northeastern corner of Oregon, the Wallowas are billed as America's "Little Switzerland," and in fact resemble the Alps geologically. Of Oregon's 31 tallest peaks, 18 are here. The town of Joseph, a gateway to the most popular trailheads at Wallowa Lake, earned its Wild West pedigree. Joseph's downtown bank was in fact robbed by bandits on horseback in 1896.

An earlier, sorrier Wild West story involves the Nez Perce tribe's Trail of Tears. In 1877, the US Army ordered the 400-member Wallowa band to move to an Idaho reservation. But a shootout just short of the reservation sent the tribe on a four-month tactical retreat, ending with defeat just 40 miles from political sanctuary in Canada. Exiled to a distant reservation, the tribe's leader, Chief Joseph, died of what his doctor called "a broken heart." Today the Nez Perce route through the harrowing chasm of Hells Canyon has been reopened for hikers and equestrians as the Nez Perce (Nee-Me-Poo) Trail. And the tribe is back, with a cultural center in the town named for its chief.

Dusty trails from the Wallowa Lake Trailhead near Joseph climb an arduous 9 miles to Lake Basin, an alpine bowl of granite-lined lakes so popular that group size is limited to six at campsites. From here a surprisingly well-graded trail switchbacks to a panoramic view at the summit of Eagle Cap. Although this 9,572-foot peak is not quite the tallest in the range, it is the rock hub of the Eagle Cap Wilderness, with river valleys radiating like spokes.

Here's a tip: Although the Lake Basin is crowded, the Wallowas have five other lake basins of matching beauty. Hike to the Pine Lakes from the ghost town of Cornucopia on the quieter, southern side of the Wallowas. Nearby, follow Eagle Creek to its source at Eagle, Bear, and Arrow Lakes. West Eagle Creek leads to a different lake cluster: Tombstone, Echo, and Traverse. A 29-mile loop from the Lostine River visits Swamp, Steamboat, and Chimney Lakes. The Wallowas have a lot of room.

Another tip: Tourists heading for the Wallowas often drive past several other magnificent mountain ranges on the way, unaware of the scenery they are overlooking. The 22.8-mile Elkhorn Crest Trail, for example, traces the craggiest part of the Blue Mountains. Because the route begins at the 7,140-foot level at Anthony Lake, you set out through the glorious sort of high-alpine meadows that hikers in the Wallowas would have to climb 3,000 feet to see.

Perhaps the prettiest driving route across Eastern Oregon follows Highway 20 past the John Day Fossil Beds, the petroglyph canyons at Picture Gorge, and the Strawberry Mountains. Pull off the highway here to hike a 15.6-mile loop around the top of that range, visiting four alpine lakes that look like calendar photos from the Canadian Rockies. A 1-mile side trail takes you to the top of 9,038-foot Strawberry Mountain itself.

For genuine adventure and solitude, however, try hiking through Hells Canyon. The gorge cut by the Snake River between Oregon and Idaho is deeper than Arizona's Grand Canyon, but—because the roads here are so poor—it's not on most tourist maps. From the end of pavement at the tumbleweed-and-rattlesnake outpost of Imnaha, you have to drive 22 miles of steep gravel to reach the trailhead at Hat Point. From there, a rough trail loses a knee-busting 5,600 feet of elevation in 7.7 miles to the Snake River. And from there, the Snake River Trail staggers faintly 49 miles downstream to the next trailhead at Dug Bar, where the road is even worse. This is no country for tenderfeet.

Eagle Cap from Mirror Lake, Eagle Cap Wilderness, Wallowa Mountains, Oregon

OREGON'S HIGH DESERT

The southeastern corner of the Oregon Country is the most remote, least populated place in the Lower 48. Set your radio to "search" and the tuner will spin in vain. The desert sky's clear, raking light seems to erase boundaries. This is freedom—a horizon empty all the way to the mountains, with your view blocked neither by buildings, nor by telephone poles, nor even by trees.

Too cold for cacti, this stark northern desert is ruled by the pungent smell of sagebrush. Where there is water—in snowmelt creeks, hot springs, and evanescent marshes—millions of migratory birds congregate. Watching whooping cranes, tundra swans, and pelicans in such a remote landscape, it's easy to wonder if these wanderers also need the clear light of the desert to feel free.

There are trails in the desert, but you don't need them. Some of the best routes follow wild horse tracks down a slot-like canyon to an alkali lakebed, or trace a ridge to the cliffy aerie of golden eagles. Start your exploration by driving southeast of the Central Oregon boomtown of Bend until the trees give out at the edge of Fort Rock Valley. Short hikes here visit oddities hidden like Easter eggs amid the sagebrush sea. Park on the rim of mile-wide Hole-in-the-Ground and follow a spiraling trail to the bottom. The gigantic crater looks like it was left by a meteorite impact, but in fact it's a volcanic maar, created when a bubble of liquid magma rose through the earth's crust, hit groundwater, and exploded.

Half a dozen miles to the east, stop at Fort Rock State Park, named for a half-mile-wide ring of cliffs that rises incongruously from desert flats. Another volcanic crater, this steep-sided "fortress" originally resembled Hole-in-the-Ground. But Fort Rock sits on a valley floor that filled with water during the wetter climate of the Ice Age years ago. Surf from the ancient lake eroded the crater's outer slope into a ring of cliffs. For proof, hike a 2-mile trailless loop around Fort Rock; the entire perimeter is notched with a "bathtub ring" left by the vanished lake's waves.

Still curious? Then drive another 20 miles east, where the roads turn to gravel, and hike through Crack-in-the-Ground. This 2-mile-long lava slot is 70 feet deep, but so narrow you sometimes have to squeeze through. The crack formed when the Four Craters Lava Field drained its underground magma reservoir and sagged, cracking the edge of a lava valley.

For even grander scenery, hike at Steens Mountain, the 9,733-foot landmark for all of southeastern Oregon. The tilted, 50-mile-long mountain rises gently from the west, but its eastern cliffs crash a vertical mile down to the Alvord Desert, Oregon's driest spot. Trails ascend gigantic U-shaped valleys carved into the crooked plateau by vanished Ice Age glaciers. The highest road in Oregon climbs almost to the summit, where rough paths lead to alpine lakes in hanging valleys.

Wilder yet are the Owyhee Canyonlands, in the forgotten world where Oregon, Nevada, and Idaho join. At Three Forks, three colossal canyons of the Owyhee River merge. Adventurers who hike into the desert labyrinth here can discover hot springs, waterfalls, caves, petroglyphs, and weirdly colored ash pinnacles that rival the marvels of national parks in Utah. But there are no park rangers here, and none of the protections that come with park status. Repeated efforts to declare the Owyhee Canyonlands a wilderness or national monument have failed. The wildest parts of the Oregon Country may be the most at risk of being lost.

Alvord Desert from Big Sand
Gap Trailhead, Oregon

WELL-KEPT SECRETS

Perhaps nowhere else on the planet are trails as diverse as in the Pacific Northwest, where hikers can choose from rain-forest jungles, alpine peaks, beach dunes, and desert canyons. Here, asking "What's your favorite trail?" is likely to make people smile. For one thing, favorites depend as much on the season as on your taste for scenery. In spring, when the rivers roar with snowmelt, you might choose a waterfall hike. Summer is the season for wildflower walks in timberline meadows. Desert mountain treks are at their best in fall, when the quaking aspen shiver with gold leaves.

It's also possible that those who smile at your question really do have a favorite trail, and won't tell. Well-kept secrets are not posted on the "top ten" lists of social media. Paths featured on Twitter and Facebook—typically near Seattle, Portland, or Bend—have become so crowded that hikers are often required to buy advance permits.

Fortunately, the Oregon Country has thousands of trails, many of them truly overlooked. This diversity gives hikers not only options, but also a responsibility to spread out away from the beaten path, to explore new trails, and to protect the wild places forgotten by the crowds. In the Pacific Northwest, the urge to hit the trail is more than a call to the freedom of the wild. It is a call to save the fragile beauty that makes the Oregon Country so rare.

Exploring Oregon *and* Northern California

PREVIOUS SPREAD: Eagle Creek Trail, Mark O. Hatfield Wilderness, Oregon

OPPOSITE: Wahclella Falls along Tanner Creek, Mark O. Hatfield Wilderness, Oregon

FOLLOWING SPREAD: Latourell Falls, Columbia River Gorge, Oregon (left); Rowena Plateau Trail toward Columbia River, Tom McCall Nature Preserve, Oregon (right)

PREVIOUS SPREAD: Trapper Lake, Sky Lakes Wilderness, Oregon

OPPOSITE: Wizard Island and Crater Lake, Crater Lake National Park, Oregon

FOLLOWING SPREAD: Upper Rogue River along Natural Bridge Loop Trail near Union Creek, Oregon (left); Camp along Rogue River Trail, Oregon (top right); Stair Creek Falls from Rogue River Trail near Inspiration Point, Wild Rogue Wilderness, Oregon (bottom right)

PREVIOUS SPREAD: Pacific Crest Trail through lodgepole pine forest, Diamond Peak Wilderness, Oregon (top left); Mount Thielsen from Tipsoo Peak, Mount Thielsen Wilderness, Oregon (bottom left); Diamond Peak reflected in Diamond View Lake, Diamond Peak Wilderness, Oregon (right)

LEFT: Mount Bachelor and Three Sisters from Big Obsidian Flow, Newberry Crater, Oregon

OPPOSITE: Broken Top, Three Sisters Wilderness, Oregon

FOLLOWING SPREAD: False hellebore and Three Fingered Jack, Mount Jefferson Wilderness, Oregon (left); Forest pond near Charlton Lake, Oregon (right)

PREVIOUS SPREAD: Pacific Crest Trail toward South Sister Mountain, Three Sisters Wilderness, Oregon (left); Mountain hemlocks with witch's hair lichen, Three Sisters Wilderness, Oregon (top right); Proxy Falls, Willamette National Forest, Oregon (bottom right)

OPPOSITE: Moonset over South Sister Mountain, Three Sisters Wilderness, Oregon

FOLLOWING SPREAD: Rock climber on Smith Rock, Smith Rock State Park, Oregon (left); Smith Rock and Crooked River from Canyon Trail, Smith Rock State Park, Oregon (right)

PREVIOUS SPREAD: Moonrise over Little Belknap Crater and Three Sisters, Mount Washington Wilderness, Oregon (left); Mount Washington, Mount Washington Wilderness, Oregon (right)

OPPOSITE: Mount Jefferson, Mount Jefferson Wilderness, Oregon

RIGHT: South Falls along Canyon Trail, Silver Falls State Park, Oregon (top); Canyon Trail, Silver Falls State Park, Oregon (bottom)

FOLLOWING SPREAD: Vine maple, Mount Jefferson Wilderness, Oregon (top left); Mountain dogwood near Lolo Pass, Oregon (bottom left); Mount Hood reflected in Mirror Lake, Mount Hood National Forest, Oregon (right)

PREVIOUS SPREAD: Jedediah
Smith Redwoods State Park,
California

OPPOSITE: Jedediah Smith
Redwoods State Park,
California

FOLLOWING SPREAD: Mount
Lassen from Chaos Crags,
Lassen Volcanic National
Park, California (left); Skylights
in Derrick Cave, Deschutes
National Forest, Oregon
(right, top and bottom)

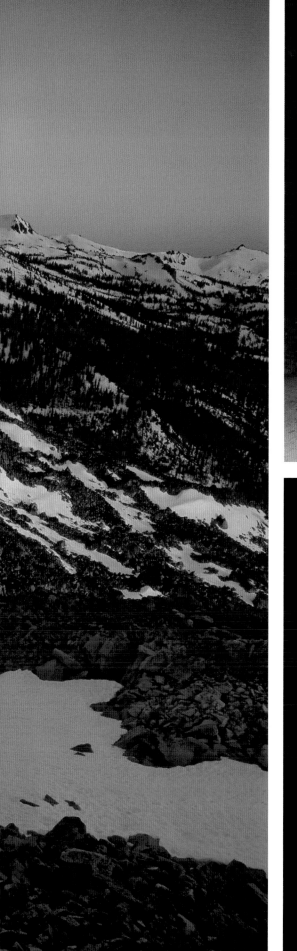

PREVIOUS SPREAD: Painted Dunes from Cinder Cone, Lassen Volcanic National Park, California (left); Cinder Cone, Lassen Volcanic National Park, California (right)

OPPOSITE: Sunrise over Baum Lake, California

FOLLOWING SPREAD: Turkey vultures from Pacific Crest Trail near Lake Britton, California (left); Burney Falls, McArthur-Burney Falls Memorial State Park, California (right)

OPPOSITE: McCloud River, Shasta-Trinity National Forest, California

RIGHT: Dogwood bloom, Castle Crags State Park, California (top); Frog beside Mosquito Creek, Trinity Alps Wilderness, California (bottom)

FOLLOWING SPREAD: Moonrise over Castle Crags, Castle Crags State Park, California (left); Lupine, Trinity Alps Wilderness, California (top right); Deer on Pacific Crest Trail, Trinity Alps Wilderness, California (bottom right)

Caesar Peak from Caribou
Lakes Trail, Trinity Alps
Wilderness, California

FOLLOWING SPREAD: Tarn in
Caribou Lakes Basin, Trinity
Alps Wilderness, California
(left); Fall color on small
shrub, Caribou Lakes Basin,
Trinity Alps Wilderness,
California (right)

Mount Shasta, Mount Shasta
Wilderness, California

FOLLOWING SPREAD: Juniper
tree and Mount Shasta
from Sheep Rock, Klamath
National Forest, California
(left); Mossbrae Falls,
Sacramento River near
Dunsmuir, California (right)

92

PREVIOUS SPREAD: Haystack Rock and Cannon Beach, Oregon Coast Trail, Oregon

OPPOSITE: View of Crescent Beach from Ecola Point, Ecola State Park, Oregon

FOLLOWING SPREAD: Short Beach access trail near Cape Meares, Oregon (top left and right); View of seagulls on rock from Short Beach near Cape Meares, Oregon (bottom left)

Devils Punchbowl, Otter
Rock, Oregon

FOLLOWING SPREAD: Sea stacks
along Bandon Beach from
Oregon Coast Trail, Oregon
(left); Whaleshead Beach,
Samuel H. Boardman State
Scenic Corridor, Oregon
(right, top and bottom)

102

PREVIOUS SPREAD: Bluebird,
Wallowa-Whitman National
Forest, Oregon (left); Hells
Canyon, Wallowa-Whitman
National Forest, Oregon
(right)

OPPOSITE: Nez Perce Trail out
of Hells Canyon, Oregon

FOLLOWING SPREAD: Eagle
Cap reflected in pond,
Lostine Meadows, Eagle
Cap Wilderness, Wallowa
Mountains, Oregon

PREVIOUS SPREAD: Glacier lily, Wallowa-Whitman National Forest, Oregon (top left); Lupine, Wallowa-Whitman National Forest, Oregon (bottom left); Falls along East Lostine River from Lostine River Trail, Eagle Cap Wilderness, Wallowa Mountains, Oregon (right)

OPPOSITE: Eagle Cap reflected in Mirror Lake, Eagle Cap Wilderness, Wallowa Mountains, Oregon

FOLLOWING SPREAD: View from near Minam Pass, Eagle Cap Wilderness, Wallowa Mountains, Oregon

PREVIOUS SPREAD: Mountain goats, Twin Lakes Trail, Blue Mountains, Oregon (left); Fort Rock, Fort Rock State Natural Area, Oregon (right)

OPPOSITE: View from Bullrun Rock toward Table Rock, Monument Rock Wilderness, Oregon

RIGHT: Indian paintbrush and lupine, Monument Rock Wilderness, Oregon (top); Mysterious cairn likely dating to the early 1900s, Monument Rock Wilderness, Oregon (bottom)

FOLLOWING SPREAD: View from Painted Hills Overlook Trail, Painted Hills Unit, John Day Fossil Beds National Monument, Oregon

PREVIOUS SPREAD: Red Hill Trail toward Red Hill, Painted Hills Unit, John Day Fossil Beds National Monument, Oregon (left); Wildflowers along Skyline Trail, Strawberry Mountain Wilderness, Strawberry Mountains, Oregon (top right); High Lake from Skyline Trail, Strawberry Mountain Wilderness, Strawberry Mountains, Oregon (bottom right)

OPPOSITE: Rock cairn along Skyline Trail, Strawberry Mountain Wilderness, Strawberry Mountains, Oregon

RIGHT: Strawberry Basin Trail toward Strawberry Lake, Strawberry Mountain Wilderness, Strawberry Mountains, Oregon

FOLLOWING SPREAD: Elkhorn Crest Trail, North Fork John Day Wilderness, Blue Mountains, Oregon (left); Strawberry Lake, Strawberry Mountain Wilderness, Strawberry Mountains, Oregon (top right); Owyhee River from near Three Forks, Owyhee Canyonlands, Oregon (bottom right)

PREVIOUS SPREAD: Wildhorse
Lake Basin from Wildhorse
Lake Trail, Steens Mountain
Wilderness, Oregon

Timber Gulch Trail, Leslie
Gulch, Oregon

PREVIOUS SPREAD: Coffeepot Crater, Jordan Craters, Oregon (top left); Trail through Crack-in-the-Ground near Christmas Valley, Oregon (bottom left); View of Alvord Desert from above Big Sand Gap Trail, Oregon (right)

Pueblo Mountains from Oregon Desert Trail, Oregon

137

WASHINGTON *and* SOUTHWESTERN BRITISH COLUMBIA

Craig Romano

The Mountain is out! This statement, recurrently heard throughout Western Washington, needs no further elaboration. Despite the region's reputation as perpetually gloomy and drizzly, the sun shines frequently in the Evergreen State. And when the skies are clear, the Mountain—that is, Mount Rainier, the Pacific Northwest's highest and most iconic peak—can be seen from much of the state. Visitors catch a glimpse of the 14,411-foot hulking volcano glistening with snow and glacial ice and feel its magical pull. Mount Rainier beckons all beholden by its beauty to get outside. And for many that means hiking.

From a wilderness coastline to craggy mountain ranges to shrub-steppe canyons, thousands of miles of trail await your boot prints. Washington is home to three national parks, 31 federal wilderness areas, and several national monuments, including one encompassing the continent's most famous active volcano, Mount St. Helens.

There's no shortage of trails to accommodate the expanding number of Washingtonians, many of whom have relocated here not for the state's booming economy, but for its vibrant natural environment. Washington's urban dwellers are never far from a trail. Seattleites can hike during their lunch break in sprawling Discovery Park, with its 10 miles of bluff-top trails. Folks in Tacoma have the old-growth forest of 760-acre Point Defiance Park to explore. And in Spokane, the 30-mile Centennial Trail winds right through downtown, passing a thundering waterfall and traversing 11,162-acre Riverside State Park, Washington's second-largest state park.

Visitors can go "*Wild*" on two long-distance national scenic trails. The Pacific Crest Trail (PCT) travels south to north for more than 500 miles along the spine of the Cascades, while the Pacific Northwest Trail travels more than 800 miles east to west on its way from the Rocky Mountains to the Olympic Mountains. The nearly 300-mile Palouse to Cascades Trail explores the state's heartland, a big-sky country of shrub-steppe hills, canyons, and plateaus.

The situation is similar just to the north in southwestern British Columbia. Throughout the Lower Mainland, where most of the province's population lives and works, imposing mountains form an emerald and snowcapped craggy backdrop to towers of steel and glass. South of the Fraser Valley, just below the 48th parallel, lies glacier-shrouded Mount Baker, and like its volcanic cousin Mount Rainier, it acts as a recreational barometer when fully revealed. North from West Vancouver to Chilliwack, rows of homes and condos abruptly yield to towering firs, steep slopes, and deep canyons—a most dramatic transition from urban to wild.

PREVIOUS SPREAD: Distant Mount Shuksan and Goat Mountain, Mount Baker Wilderness, Washington

Mount Baker and flower field along Skyline Divide, Mount Baker Wilderness, Washington

Vancouverites and Victorians have trails, mountains, and fjords accessible to them at the end of a transit line. Large provincial parks rivaling American national parks and forests in size protect huge swaths of British Columbia's North Cascades, Coast Ranges, and Vancouver Island Mountains. Dramatic waterfalls, massive ice fields, ancient cathedral forests, and glacial cirques teeming with shimmering alpine lakes are all accessible by a good and growing trail network, and all within a short drive for most British Columbians and many of their Washington neighbors.

Meander, amble, saunter, or skedaddle down any of Washington's or southwestern British Columbia's trails and embrace the region's natural, historical, and cultural heritage. Follow paths built by Native Americans for hunting and trading and later used by European, American, and Canadian trappers, explorers, and settlers. Explorers George Vancouver, David Thompson, Lewis and Clark, Simon Fraser, and Charles Wilkes left their mark on the land in the form of place names and setting the way for future development, but the region also fostered a pioneering outdoors culture, leaving its mark on the land through the creation of sprawling parks, preserves, and vast networks of trails.

OLYMPIC PENINSULA

The serrated, snowcapped Olympic Mountains across Puget Sound's shimmering waters create a dramatic backdrop for Seattle's sparkling skyline. From the city's waterfront, they practically breathe down upon you. Yet this range was among the last in the Lower 48 to be explored by European Americans. By the late 1800s, Canadian explorer James Christie and US Army Second Lieutenant Joseph P. O'Neil were racing to be the first to traverse the Olympic Peninsula's forbidding interior.

Christie's Press Expedition (sponsored by the *Seattle Press*) got a head start in the fall of 1889. Making a grueling north-to-south traverse, the men successfully reached the coast in May 1890. O'Neil's expedition (sponsored by the US Army and William Gladstone Steel, who later founded Mazamas, the Portland-based outdoors club) successfully traversed the peninsula from east to west the following summer.

Both parties blazed trails, climbed mountains, and documented geographic and natural features along the way. They bestowed names on rivers, peaks, and other landmarks. But it was O'Neil who stated in 1896 that these mountains would serve admirably as a national park. Thirteen years later, President Theodore Roosevelt, alarmed by the overhunting of the region's elk herds, proclaimed the area a national monument.

Today, backpackers can trace Christie's and O'Neil's historic routes on well-maintained trails. Astute travelers may even notice blazes left behind from the intrepid explorers.

Hike O'Neil's route by following the North Fork Skokomish River through a deep valley, over a divide, and then up to a handful of sparkling subalpine lakes in LaCrosse Basin, where bear and elk outnumber hikers.

Continue over O'Neil Pass to the East Fork Quinault River's Enchanted Valley, also known as the Valley of 1,000 Waterfalls. Hyperbolic? Just a tad. Exit the valley near Lake Quinault, set in a primeval rain forest and home to an elegant lodge. In 1937, President Franklin D. Roosevelt stayed here on a trip that convinced him to create Olympic National Park nine months later. In 1988, 95 percent of the park's 920,000 acres were declared wilderness—the largest in the state.

PREVIOUS SPREAD: Madrone tree overlooking Puget Sound, Fragrance Lake Trail, Larrabee State Park, Washington

Suspension bridge over North Fork Skokomish River, Olympic National Park, Washington

To follow Christie's route, hike 44 miles up the Elwha Valley, over the Low Divide, and down the North Fork Quinault Valley. Pass old homesteads, a dramatic chasm named Goblins Gate, and one of the largest tracts of ancient forest remaining in the country. Witness the rebirth of the Elwha River, where two recently removed dams are returning salmon runs and delivering renewed hope to the Klallam people, whose ancestors subsisted on the once-prolific fish stocks.

Near the mouth of the Elwha River rises Hurricane Ridge, with its 17-mile winding road that allows hikers to probe the Olympic high country. Set out on trails across mile-high meadows bursting with dazzling wildflowers and rife with jaw-dropping views of glistening Mount Olympus, the highest and snowiest peak on the peninsula. Embrace close-up panoramas of the mountain from the High Divide, a flowered open ridge cradling the legendary Seven Lakes Basin. Share the stunning surroundings with endemic Olympic marmots and ubiquitous black bears, which are drawn to the bounteous huckleberry patches.

Processions of storms rolling off of the Pacific Ocean barrage the Olympics' western flanks, resulting in some of the wettest valleys on the planet. Hike through saturated temperate rain forests in the Humptulips, Quinault, Queets, Hoh, and Bogachiel Valleys to arboreal giants rivaling the redwoods in age and size. Follow the Hoh River Trail through glades of moss-draped maples and groves of purplish scaly-barked spruces all the way to the icy toe of the Blue Glacier snaking down from Mount Olympus.

In the 1950s, Congress added a 73-mile coastal strip to Olympic National Park, protecting one of the wildest coastlines remaining in the continental United States. From Lake Ozette, hike a 9.5-mile triangular loop passing centuries-old petroglyphs and prairies where tenacious homesteaders ultimately succumbed to unrelenting rain. Hike past the site of a Makah village that was buried by a mudslide nearly 500 years ago. Visit the Makah Museum on the Makah Reservation to see artifacts from the site. Then hike to Cape Flattery, a dramatic headland protruding into tumultuous waters where the Strait of Juan de Fuca meets the Pacific Ocean. The northwesternmost point in the continental United States, it provides an excellent vantage for spotting seals, whales, and pelagic birds riding swells.

Near the Quileute Reservation, hike to sea stacks and a natural arch at Second Beach or to a waterfall crashing into the pounding surf at Third Beach. The 2-mile hike to Hole-in-the-Wall at Rialto Beach is a popular haunt for *Twilight* fans searching for attractive vampires. The 17-mile trek to Toleak Point's sea stacks, middens, and lonely sweeping beaches involves strenuous climbing via sand ladders over steep headlands. The effort is worth it to witness in solitude a restless ocean extinguishing the sun at day's end.

SOUTH CASCADES

"If the mountain goes, I'm going with it," quipped Harry Truman (no relation to the president) in the spring of 1980. The curmudgeonly World War I vet and owner of a lodge on Spirit Lake within the shadows of Mount St. Helens refused to evacuate his property despite an imminent eruption. Then, on May 18, at 8:32 a.m., David Johnston, a young USGS volcanologist perched on a nearby ridge facing the volcano, famously radioed, "Vancouver! Vancouver! This is it!"

The eruption came as a lateral blast hurling debris at 300 miles per hour. Johnston instantly perished. Truman and his 16 cats were buried under a pyroclastic flow. Mount St. Helens spewed more

Mount Carrie and Mount Olympus from Hurricane Hill, Olympic National Park, Washington

than 520 million tons of ash and caused midday darkness across the state. Destructive lahars swept away all in their paths. The eruption killed 57 people, nearly all wildlife on the mountain, and every tree within a 6-mile radius. The peak once referred to as the Mount Fuji of America lost more than 1,300 feet of its top.

Mount St. Helens, like California's Lassen Peak 65 years earlier, reaffirmed that the Cascades are an active mountain range. Washington's South Cascades teem with testaments to the power of volcanism. The region is pocked with craters and shrouded with old lava flows. And nearly every trail traversing this region grants views of impressive volcanoes: feisty Mount St. Helens, juggernaut Mount Rainier, flat-topped Mount Adams, and the craggy Goat Rocks—the remnant caldera of a massive extinct volcano.

Two years after the famous eruption, Congress designated the 110,000-acre Mount St. Helens National Volcanic Monument. Crews rebuilt trails and constructed miles of new tread. The nearly 30-mile rough-and-tumble Loowit Trail (the Yakama and Klickitat peoples' name for the volcano, meaning "smoking mountain") circumnavigates Mount St. Helens, revealing old lava flows, flowered meadows, stark pumice plains, and luxuriant primeval forests that escaped the blast. The monument's Mount Margaret Backcountry took a full hit from the 1980 eruption, but it's no wasteland. Nature is recolonizing the region with a vengeance, and elk and wildflowers are prolific.

Via the Lakes Trail, traverse the blast zone, passing a series of stunning lakes tucked into remote basins. Follow the Boundary Trail to Norway Pass and gaze out at Spirit Lake, with its shifting flotillas of silvery old-growth logs against a dramatic backdrop of the volcano. Not for the faint of heart, the Whittier Ridge Trail travels along knife edges and across narrow ledges blasted into sheer cliffs where only mountain goats and intrepid hikers dare to go.

Secure a permit and make the 5-mile grunt up pumiced slopes littered with basaltic boulders to Mount St. Helens's summit. Stare straight into the crater to an expanding glacier feeding a stunning waterfall. Look out to Mounts Rainier, Adams, Hood, and Jefferson—giant snowy sentinels that shaped and continue to shape the topography around them.

Further explore that topography by following the PCT. Skirt the 8-mile-long Big Lava Bed and then enter the Indian Heaven Wilderness, a high plateau pocked with more than 150 small lakes and, in summer, millions of mosquitoes. Consider visiting in autumn for its billions of berries. Marvel at the Racetrack, where area tribes once met to race horses, and climb Sawtooth Mountain for a marvelous view of Washington's second-highest summit, 12,281-foot Mount Adams.

Sacred to the Yakama people and known as Pahto ("high sloping mountain"), Mount Adams was once the site of a sulfur mine and the state's highest fire lookout. Its ascent is straightforward and nontechnical, but not so the hike around the mountain. Treacherous ravines housing thundering rivers on the mountain's eastern flanks prohibit the Round-the-Mountain Trail from truly traveling around the mountain. Devils Garden and Adams Creek Meadows, rife with flowers and mountain goats, are worthy objectives along the route.

North of Mount Adams is the sprawling 108,000-acre Goat Rocks Wilderness. The PCT reaches its highest elevation north of the Sierras here along a knife-edge crest, and wildflowers are legendary at Snowgrass Flats. Scramble up Old Snowy, a precipitous point on the ancient volcanic crest, for jaw-slacking

Mount St. Helens from
Pacific Crest Trail near
Indian Heaven Wilderness,
Washington

views of bookend volcanos Adams and Rainier. Goat Lake harbors ice throughout the summer, and the verdant slopes above it are often blotched white with grazing mountain goats.

The PCT crosses White Pass to enter the William O. Douglas Wilderness, named for the Yakima son who became the longest-serving US Supreme Court justice. A staunch advocate for civil rights and the environment, Douglas maintained a cabin at Goose Prairie, now surrounded by the wilderness. Hike to some of his favorite haunts—Twin Lakes and Cougar Lakes—or scores of other lakes dotting a broad plateau. Ascend Tumac Mountain, an extinct volcanic cinder cone, or clamber up 7,766-foot Mount Aix. The supreme views of Mount Rainier hovering over the William O. country from these former lookout sites are worth the toil.

MOUNT RAINIER

At 14,411 feet, Mount Rainier ("Tahoma" to the Coast Salish peoples) is the highest mountain in the Pacific Northwest. An active stratovolcano harboring more than 25 glaciers, Mount Rainier is the snowiest mountain in the Lower 48. Its most impressive attribute, however, is its 13,200 feet of topographic prominence. It is the most prominent peak in the continental United States; on a clear day, the glistening volcano can be seen hovering on the horizon from much of the state.

Prized by climbers, the long and growing list of Mount Rainier summiteers includes quite an impressive roster dating back to 1870. Conservationist John Muir made the ascent in 1888. And while Muir was impressed with being on the mountain, he felt that it was better appreciated from below. He saw the value in preserving the area's vast old-growth forests and pristine alpine meadows. Thanks in part to his writings, in 1899 the mountain became America's fifth national park.

Folks from all over the world come to witness extravagant floral arrangements by hiking easy, short, paved paths—or longer, grander trails—from Mount Rainier's appositely named Paradise Valley. The 5.6-mile Skyline Trail loops through alpine meadows, glacial moraine, snowfields, and across cascading creeks, all while providing jaw-dropping views of the snowy volcano and the serrated Tatoosh Range. Hikers can follow the Lakes Trail 2 miles to a procession of photographers with tripods intent on capturing the mountain perfectly mirrored in the Reflection Lakes.

Mount Rainier's summit is strictly for climbers, but when conditions are agreeable experienced strong hikers can trudge 4.5 arduous miles up glistening snowfields to Camp Muir at 10,188 feet. The real lure for hikers, however, is the Wonderland Trail. Constructed in 1915, it's one of the most beautiful, challenging, and popular hiking trails in America. Traveling 93 miles around the mountain, and gaining more than 25,000 feet of elevation along the way, it traverses primeval forests, alpine meadows, alpine tundra, subalpine lakeshores, snowfields, and glacial moraine—in essence, every life zone within the 235,000-plus-acre national park.

Most hikers take seven to 10 days to complete the circuit, and securing permits for the journey can be as challenging as completing the trail. But numerous access points allow for satisfying day hikes on the Wonderland Trail. At Indian Henry's Hunting Ground, marvel at meadows of dazzling wildflowers and subalpine pools that reflect an array of Mount Rainier's fierce rock faces and glaciers and admire a 1915

Mount Rainier reflected in a tarn, Spray Park, Mount Rainier National Park, Washington

patrol cabin, the oldest in the park. Indian Henry (So-To-Lick) was believed by many area settlers to have a gold mine somewhere on the mountain. The mine was never found, but scenic riches abound.

Views of Little Tahoma, a volcanic remnant on Mount Rainier, are exhilarating from Summerland, where a stone shelter built by the Civilian Conservation Corps (CCC) sits at the edge of high meadows. The 3.2-mile hike to Tolmie Peak from Mowich Lake, the largest lake in the park, is a popular family outing. En route, pass walls of columnar basalt and the shores of sparkling Eunice Lake beneath Tolmie's rocky south face. Then, reach the 1933 fire lookout on the peak and stand mesmerized while gazing at two shimmering lakes before Mount Rainier.

The 8-mile Spray Park Trail from Mowich Lake is beautiful, but potentially dangerous due to its permanent snowfield crossings. It passes a 350-foot waterfall and legendary parkland meadows on its way to the Carbon River Valley. Hike 8 miles up the abandoned Carbon River Road through interior rain forest harboring groves of cathedral trees. Then, continue 3 miles on the Wonderland Trail along the channeled Carbon River to a 200-plus-foot suspension bridge spanning the river near the Carbon Glacier, the lowest glacier in the continental United States.

The Sunrise area sits at an elevation of 6,400 feet. Thanks to Mount Rainier's rain-shadow effect, Sunrise is considerably drier than the Paradise area. An excellent network of trails radiates from the Sunrise Visitor Center to dazzling meadows, open pine forests, and peaks and ridges graced with close-up views of the mountain.

Hike 2.7 miles to a fire lookout perched on rocky Mount Fremont. At nearly 7,200 feet, this historic structure is the highest of the park's four lookouts. Savor in-your-face views of the impressive Willis Wall and massive Emmons Glacier, and look north over Grand Park, a near-level, nearly 2-mile-long emerald expanse of meadows. For even closer views of Mount Rainier, traipse up alpine tundra and snowfields to Burroughs Mountain's trio of exposed summits.

Four national forest wilderness areas border the periphery of the park. All contain excellent trails to stunning vistas, lakes, and summits, but with far fewer hikers than the park receives. Hike 2.4 miles to Mount Beljica, a small but pronounced peak in the Glacier View Wilderness, and savor stupendous views of long ribbons of glacial ice streaking down Mount Rainier's frosty western face.

The only thing more gorgeous than the wildflowers carpeting the craggy knolls and pyramidal peaks in the Tatoosh Wilderness are the views of snow-white Mount Rainier looming over them. Hike 5.2 miles across steep slopes to an old lookout site shadowing two tiny tarns in a frozen basin. The lookout was made famous by schoolteacher Martha Hardy, who wrote about her experiences working as a fire keep here in 1943 in her book *Tatoosh*. She was one of just a few female lookouts at a time when many working men had enlisted to fight in World War II.

ISSAQUAH ALPS

Named by renowned guidebook author, conservationist, and trails advocate Harvey Manning, the Issaquah Alps consist of a series of forested Cascades Foothills minutes from downtown Seattle. Once the domain of loggers and miners, the Issaquah Alps—thanks in large part to Manning's dogged advocacy—are one of the largest urban wildlands in America and a key component of the Mountains to Sound Greenway.

Alarmed by encroaching urban sprawl in the 1990s, a large contingent of folks called for the Issaquah Alps and adjacent farmlands, valleys, forests, and communities along the I-90 corridor from Seattle to Ellensburg to be included in a Mountains to Sound Greenway. The effort was spearheaded by the Mountains to Sound Greenway Trust, and more than 900,000 acres in the greenway are now publicly owned, with an additional 100,000 acres conserved as private working forests. In 2019, the area was designated by Congress as a national heritage area to encourage its historic preservation.

Within an hour's drive for four million people, the Issaquah Alps contain some of the busiest trails in the state. But with more than 100 miles of well-built trails traversing more than 25,000 acres of public lands, there's plenty of room for everyone. Cougar Mountain is the lowest and closest to Seattle of the Issaquah Alps, and the most interesting when it comes to human history. Coal discovered here in the 1860s by early European Americans led to settlements and a flourishing coal industry. From 1957 to 1964, the US military ran a Nike missile base on the mountain. In the 1980s, the area was transformed into King County's largest park.

From Cougar Mountain's Red Town Trailhead, hike through the remains of an old mining town before setting out on a 4.8-mile loop up and over De Leo Wall, with its stately trees and views out to Mount Rainier and Lake Washington. It's an easy 2.5-mile round-trip hike to Coal Creek Falls, the crown jewel of the sprawling Cougar Mountain Regional Wildland Park. The 28-foot cascade tumbles over mossy

Wildflower garden near Chinook Pass, Mount Rainier National Park, Washington (left); Carbon Glacier from above Mystic Lake, Mount Rainier National Park, Washington (right)

ledges and is especially delightful after autumn rains swell the creek and golden maple leaves brighten the surrounding emerald gorge.

Tiger Mountain consists of several peaks, with the tallest just exceeding 3,000 feet. The bulk of this peak lies within a 13,745-acre state forest containing more than 60 miles of trails. At Tradition Plateau, explore more than 8 miles of easy trails traversing quiet woodlots, wetlands, and lakeshores. Nothing stinks about Tiger Mountain's Poo Poo Point, which was named for the sound emitted by old logging operations' steam whistles. From this open grassy spot revered by paragliders, relish excellent views of Lake Sammamish before the Bellevue skyline. One of Washington's most popular hikes, Poo Poo—with its 1,650-foot elevation gain in 1.9 miles—is no walk in the park.

Squak Mountain is situated between popular Tiger and Cougar Mountains and is often overlooked by hikers. Forming a green backdrop to the high-tech suburb of Issaquah, trails lead right from the city up this forgotten Alp.

At an elevation of 3,500 feet, Rattlesnake Mountain is the highest of the Issaquah Alps. However, most hikers (and there are legions) only hike the 2.1 miles to its famous ledges. From these precipitous ledges overlooking deep-blue Rattlesnake Lake, enjoy a sweeping view of three grand glacier-scoured valleys along the Cascade front.

ALPINE LAKES

Teeming with more than 700 lakes and 600 miles of trails traversing more than 400,000 acres of rugged mountains, deep glacier-carved valleys, and primeval forests—all within a one-hour drive of Seattle—it's no surprise that the Alpine Lakes are one of the most popular wilderness areas in the country. A true backyard wilderness for millions of people, many of its periphery trails act as gateways to more serious adventuring for multitudes of budding hikers.

Despite their serious elevation gain, towering sentinels Mount Si and Mailbox Peak on the Cascades front are two of the most-climbed mountains in the state. Hikers who endure the 5.5-mile, 4,000-foot climb to Mailbox get to revel on the summit with a selfie at a real mailbox stuffed with eclectic offerings. Thanks to citizen groups like the Washington Trails Association (WTA) and Mountains to Sound Greenway Trust, the once-neglected Middle Fork Snoqualmie River Valley has been rejuvenated into a family-friendly destination rife with resurrected and brand-new trails.

I-90 provides quick access to some of the state's prettiest front country. Plan an early start to beat the crowds to Mason Lake on the Ira Spring Trail, named for a conservationist and renowned photographer who, along with his twin brother and WTA founder Louise Marshall, produced a pioneering guidebook in 1966 introducing folks to many of the state's backcountry trails. Spring later collaborated with wilderness advocate Harvey Manning to produce a voluminous array of guidebooks bringing awareness to the state's threatened wild places and instilling advocacy to protect them.

Snoqualmie Pass's Snow Lake sees no shortage of hikers making the 3-mile trek to witness stark walls, spiraling summits, and perpetual snowfields reflecting upon its deep, clear waters. The PCT goes through Snoqualmie Pass, traveling 75 miles across the Alpine Lakes Wilderness on its way to Stevens

Mailbox at top of Mailbox Peak, Cascades, Washington

"It isn't enough to have just a few righteous people talking about preserving trails. We need a lot of them."
–Ira Spring

This trail was built with nearly 10,000 hours of volunteer labor from the Mountains to Sound Greenway Trust, Washington Trails Association, EarthCorps, Washington Conservation Corps, Washington State Department of Natural Resources, REI, and others.

We are grateful for their work.

Pass. Known as Section J, this stretch of the PCT is a popular backpacking route. It passes classic spots like the Kendall Katwalk, a dynamite-blasted passageway across sheer granite cliffs; nearly 2-mile-long Waptus Lake, the largest lake in the wilderness; and aptly named Spectacle Lake, with its numerous fingers of polished ledge sheltering placid inlets reflecting shiny granite turrets.

Trails originating from Highway 2 along the wilderness's northern flanks see considerably less use than ones from I-90. Follow trails here for a few miles—or several days—up deep valleys to chains of sparkling lakes. Surrounded by centuries-old ancient forests and shiny rocky ledges scoured by ancient ice floes, Lake Dorothy would still be a popular destination if the hike were twice as long as its 1.75 miles.

Tucked in basins and rocky cirques high above the West Fork Foss River is a bevy of big, beautiful alpine lakes—one of the highest concentrations of lakes within the entire Alpine Lakes Wilderness. You could spend weeks exploring Copper, Little Heart, Big Heart, Angeline, Chetwoot, and other shimmering bodies of water. Nearby Necklace Valley is another backpacking jewel. Hike 9 miles through deep forests and up steep, rocky, taxing slopes to a crashing cascade careening from the edge of a hanging valley. Then explore a strand of aquatic alpine gems strung together in a tight valley shadowed by craggy summits and sheer rock faces.

The Teanaway Country in the wilderness's southeastern corner is blessed with ample sunshine and resplendent wildflower gardens. Home to rare endemics and showy blossoms, many a west-side hiker makes an annual summer pilgrimage here. In autumn, they return to see aspens and larches set the slopes aglow in gold. Hike 5 rugged miles to Lake Ingalls, cradled in a high barren basin beneath the rocky facade of Ingalls Peak. When its icy waters lay calm, capturing reflections of 9,415-foot Mount Stuart's sheer rock face, the view is striking.

The Enchantment Lakes are the most sought-after terrain in the Alpine Lakes. Set in a hanging valley beneath Mount Stuart, the "Chants" are a legendary place of shiny granite, sparkling waters, glistening snowfields, prolific herds of mountain goats, and golden larches in autumn. The 19-mile one-way hike through them via Colchuck Lake—with its turquoise waters and the intimidating notched portal Aasgard Pass—is a Pacific Northwest classic. So popular and fragile is this area, however, that the Forest Service has enacted restrictive rules and a limited permit system for those wishing to overnight here. Every spring hikers eagerly await to hear if they've won the lottery for a coveted permit.

NORTH CASCADES

"Hozomeen, Hozomeen, most beautiful mountain I've ever seen," waxed Jack Kerouac from the top of 6,102-foot Desolation Peak. The Beatnik poet spent 63 days in the summer of 1956 staffing a fire lookout on this isolated summit in the heart of some of the most spectacular alpine scenery on the planet. It's a long 21-mile hike to this peak, or you can catch a water taxi to shorten it. But the views—from fjord-like Ross Lake's cobalt waters lined with glacier-shrouded peaks to Kerouac's muse, 8,066-foot Hozomeen Mountain and its fearsome twin sheer-vertical spires—are truly inspirational.

The North Cascades are impressive and formidable. Draped in ice, they contain half the glaciers in the Lower 48. Affectionately referred to as America's Alps, they were recognized as national park caliber

Chetwoot Lake, Alpine Lakes Wilderness, Washington

by early conservationists. In 1968, after years of fighting entrenched timber and mining interests, nearly 700,000 acres were protected as the North Cascades National Park and adjacent Ross Lake and Lake Chelan National Recreation Areas.

The North Cascades Highway, a national scenic byway, traverses the region and provides access to spellbinding trails. The 7.2-mile Maple Pass Loop transcends various life zones culminating in alpine tundra. Relish resplendent alpine meadows showcasing a kaleidoscope of colors, and amble along high, open ridges delighting in a surrounding skyline of serrated summits.

The Cascade Pass Trail follows a route used by Native Americans, explorers, prospectors, and surveyors to reach Lake Chelan. From the base of a daunting wall of jagged icy summits, the 3.7-mile trail switchbacks some 30 times en route to the pass. Trudge farther up Sahale Arm, domain to gregarious marmots, hiking all the way to the heavens or to the Sahale Glacier—whichever you reach first. Hike east of Cascade Pass to Stehekin (population 75) on the northwestern tip of 50-mile-long Lake Chelan. This remote community can only be reached by plane, boat, or trail.

At the North Cascades' western reaches, follow Mount Baker Highway to Heather Meadows, a subalpine wonderland of hemlock hugging hillocks and sparkling lakes set beneath barren slopes cloaked in snow and ice. Between two North Cascades iconic peaks—9,131-foot Mount Shuksan, one of the most photographed mountains in the country, and 10,778-foot Mount Baker, Washington's third-highest and snowiest summit—set out on paved paths for easy ambling or rougher trails for challenging clambering.

Hike the 7.3-mile Chain Lakes Loop around snow- and ice-clad Table Mountain to a half-dozen shimmering alpine lakes. Delight in summer blossoms, autumn berries, and the year-round scenic splendor of Mounts Shuksan and Baker forming two frosty bookend giants. On Mount Baker (which Native Americans called Koma Kulshan, "the white sentinel"), hike 3.6 miles to the historic Park Butte fire lookout, or follow the Skyline Divide Trail for 4.5 miles across flower-saturated meadows above glistening snowfields. It was on Mount Baker in 1906 that W. Montelius Price and renowned photographer Asahel Curtis conceived a Seattle-based mountaineering club. The following year they broke away from the Portland-based Mazamas and established The Mountaineers. Out of its 151 charter members, 77 were women.

The half-million-plus-acre Pasayten Wilderness encompasses much of the North Cascades' northeastern reaches. Follow the Boundary Trail (part of the Pacific Northwest Trail) 73 miles across the vast wilderness, traversing windswept ridges carpeted with alpine tundra and passing larch-ringed lakes tucked in dramatic cirques. Watch for lynx and listen for wolves in this roadless area along the Canadian border.

The PCT traverses the North Cascades from south to north. From Stevens Pass, follow it into the Henry M. Jackson Wilderness, named for a long-serving senator and environmental champion, and into the adjacent sprawling 566,000-acre Glacier Peak Wilderness. Hike along high ridges undulating between primeval forests and resplendent alpine meadows, lured by majestic snowy, showy 10,541-foot Glacier Peak.

Divert from the PCT to Image Lake on Miners Ridge. You haven't experienced the full grandeur of the North Cascades until you've witnessed morning's first rays of sunlight—or evening's fading light—waltzing across the snow and ice of Washington's most remote volcano perfectly reflected upon Image Lake's placid waters.

Pacific Crest Trail through meadow near White Pass, Glacier Peak Wilderness, Washington

FOLLOWING SPREAD: Image Lake and Glacier Peak, Glacier Peak Wilderness, Washington

Beyond, the PCT crosses the Stehekin Valley and North Cascades Highway, reaching Harts Pass, accessed by the highest road in Washington, a twisting narrow dirt road built in 1893 to reach nearby gold and silver mines. The PCT proceeds through a plethora of passes on its way to its northern terminus in British Columbia's E. C. Manning Provincial Park. There's no shortage of excellent trails to explore in 200,000-plus-acre Manning and adjacent Skagit Valley Provincial Park and Cascade Recreation Area.

From a lofty start, follow the Heather Trail across a rolling subalpine wonderland. After ambling 6.5 miles across sprawling meadows that blossom in a riot of colors, reach the summit of the first of the Three Brothers. From the Skyline Trail, stare straight down at Thunder Lake wedged between steep slopes stripped of vegetation from endless processions of avalanches. And avert your eyes outward to the stark, rocky spires of Hozomeen Mountain, which entranced and enlightened Kerouac. The 13-mile round-trip hike to 7,900-foot Frosty Mountain, the park's highest summit, includes a trip through one of Canada's oldest forests—a stand of alpine larches with trees close to 2,000 years old—before culminating with breathtaking views of Washington sentinels.

East of E. C. Manning Provincial Park and bordering the sprawling Pasayten Wilderness is Cathedral Provincial Park, home to Canada's highest full-service hiking lodge. From its location on Quiniscoe Lake at 6,800 feet, head out on trails traversing the Cathedral Rim. Clamber through scree and across alpine tundra following lichen-encrusted cairns to summits exceeding 8,300 feet. Admire a half-dozen alpine lakes twinkling below in cliffy amphitheaters, and marvel at fascinating rock formations along the rim: the Devil's Woodpile, an outcropping of columnar basalt; Stone City, rounded rocks resembling giant curling stones piled on top of each other; and Smokey the Bear, a large, sheer cliff face.

Where the North Cascades meet the arid Okanagan Valley, hike an easy 2.6-mile loop on Mount Kobau's broad summit, savoring sweeping, jaw-dropping views encompassing snowy summits and sunbaked steppe. Gaze at a line of summits straddling the international boundary and soaring nearly 7,000 feet above the Similkameen Valley. It's one of the most dramatic reliefs in North America. Mount Kobau's threatened sage shrub ecosystem is home to 30 federal species at risk. Parks Canada has been working with a coalition of folks and the Syilx Okanagan Nation to establish here a South Okanagan-Similkameen National Park.

VANCOUVER ISLAND

In 1907, one year after the steamship *Valencia* horrifically went down in the treacherous waters off Vancouver Island's wild and isolated West Coast, claiming 136 lives, the Canadian government constructed the Dominion Lifesaving Trail to aid the rescue of shipwrecked seafarers. Now known as the West Coast Trail, folks come from around the world to backpack this challenging 47-mile route along one of the most ruggedly spectacular shorelines in the Pacific Northwest.

While the trail is now managed by the Pacific Rim National Park Reserve through a partnership with the Pacheedaht, Ditidaht, and Huu-ay-aht First Nations (whose ancestral lands the trail traverses), it's still rough and hazardous, warranting more than 100 rescues every year. The number of West Coast Trail hikers are restricted, and an orientation session is required before departure. The grueling journey

West Coast Trail, Carmanah Walbran Provincial Park, Vancouver Island, British Columbia includes river fords and cable-car crossings, taxing boggy and rooty terrain, more than 100 ladders, and often incessant rains and howling winds. Perseverance is rewarded with unsurpassed beauty: the trail passes hidden sandy beaches, coastal waterfalls, primeval rain forest, remote lighthouses, historic First Nations' village sites, and nearly 80 shipwreck sites, giving this stretch of coastline the moniker "Graveyard of the Pacific."

Backpackers unsuccessful at receiving a West Coast Trail permit can venture on the nearby and less arduous Juan de Fuca Marine Trail. This 29-mile trail can also be day hiked in sections thanks to

four trailheads. Hike across suspension bridges and alongside sheer coastal cliffs. Explore sandstone and basaltic shelves teeming with rich tide pools, watch for gray whales and orcas plying the surf, and feast on breathtaking views across the Strait of Juan de Fuca to Washington's Olympic Mountains.

British Columbians living in or near the capital city of Victoria have access to hundreds of miles of nearby trails. East Sooke Regional Park's 6.2-mile Coast Trail will have you clambering and scrambling between stunning viewpoints of snowy Olympic Mountain peaks. Head to the sprawling Gowlland Tod Provincial Park next to the world-famous Butchart Gardens, and hike across the Gowlland Range, with its breathtaking views into Finlayson Arm, a dramatic 1,300-foot fjord. The Cowichan Valley Trail leads across the wooden 1920 Kinsol Trestle, which spans more than 600 feet and towers nearly 150 feet above the Koksilah River. It's one of the highest railway trestles in the world.

Ancestral home to 50 First Nations, Vancouver Island became a British colony in 1849, six years after the Hudson's Bay Company's Fort Victoria was established. Since European settlement, only 20 percent of the immense island's grand old-growth forests remain. The 1990s brought international attention to the island, leading to the protection of exceptional primeval forests in the Carmanah Valley. Drive a bumpy 50-mile logging road to the 40,000-acre Carmanah Walbran Provincial Park and hike through cathedral forests containing trees of unconceivable proportions. Stroll through groves of 800-year-old Sitka spruces, towering more than 300 feet high and rivaling California's redwoods.

Vancouver Island's largest protected area is the 614,475-acre Strathcona Provincial Park, which was established in 1911 as British Columbia's first provincial park. The park contains the highest peak on the island—7,201-foot Golden Hinde—other glacier-capped mountains, thundering waterfalls, primeval forests, and scores of alpine lakes. The park is inhabited by wolves, white-tailed ptarmigans, and recovering populations of the endemic Vancouver Island marmot, one of the most endangered mammals in Canada.

Much of the park is wilderness, but it also contains some of the best hiking trails on the island. The Flower Ridge Trail wastes no time climbing nearly 5,000 feet to a rolling open ridge rife with wildflowers, tarns, and jaw-dropping views of some of the park's grandest features, including fjord-like Buttle Lake, the massive Comox Glacier, and Nine Peaks hovering over Cream Lake. Arrange a water taxi up Great Central Lake and hike 10 miles up a deep valley to Della Falls, which crashes 1,443 feet to the valley floor, making it one of the highest waterfalls in Canada. The park's Forbidden Plateau offers exceptional hiking for all levels and extensive overnight options with its backcountry campsites. From a trailhead at 3,500 feet, amble along sparkling alpine lakes, across wildflower meadows, and up alpine tundra to rocky Mount Albert Edward with its awe-inspiring views. And don't worry about the plateau's lore of evil spirits eating women and children—it was all fabricated by a 19th-century newspaperman.

COAST RANGES

From along the Cunningham Seawall Trail in Vancouver's stately Stanley Park, the view of the elegant 1930s Lions Gate Bridge spanning across the First Narrows of Burrard Inlet is a Pacific Northwest classic. Follow the Seawall east to Canada Place, and the view is greatly enhanced when the Lions, two prominent granite domes, emerge from the emerald canopy that cloaks the craggy North Shore Mountains.

Botanical Beach, Juan de Fuca Marine Trail, Botanical Beach Provincial Park, Vancouver Island, British Columbia

The Lions are among the most recognizable of the spires forming the booming city's backdrop. From Cypress Provincial Park, head north on the rough-and-tumble Howe Sound Crest Trail across the eastern rooftop of Vancouver's backyard fjord, Howe Sound. After 6 miles, reach the base of the fearsome couchant West Lion. To the Squamish people, the Lions are known as the Two Sisters, and according to legend, they were responsible for bringing the warring Squamish and Haida tribes together in peace. The 18-mile Howe Sound Trail continues north, intersecting feeder trails that brutally descend more than 5,000 feet. Along this crest, stunning views of saltwater straits and sounds and white-capped ridges above deep verdant valleys don't come easy.

East of the Lions are the iconic Golden Ears. Whether named for golden eagles or what the twin pyramidal peaks resemble when absorbing sunset's light, the Golden Ears are an impressive and imposing landmark in the Lower Mainland. The 7.7-mile hike to the North Ear is arduous, involving a rocky old logging road, 5,000 feet of vertical climbing, and a potentially treacherous snowfield crossing. But standing on top of this pinnacle dividing two glacial troughs cradling long slender lakes is enthralling. And if the lakes don't slacken your jaw, the massive snowcapped Mount Baker across the Fraser Valley in Washington will.

Nearly all of the summits north of the Golden Ears are inaccessible to all but the hardiest mountaineers. British Columbia's Coast Range is crossed by few roads and trails, and the mountains' junglelike rain-forest valleys, precipitous slopes, and massive ice fields make them among North America's most forbidding places. To the west, however, along the Sea to Sky Highway from Vancouver to the resort town of Whistler, scores of trails lead to sparkling alpine lakes, wilderness valleys, and spectacular summits.

Explore excellent trail networks emanating from Mount Seymour and Cypress Provincial Parks. The latter was created through the advocacy of the British Columbia Mountaineering Club (BCMC). Formed in 1907, the same year as Seattle's Mountaineers, the BCMC was also a pioneer in gender equality, electing a woman to its vice presidency. The club has a long history of fighting for wildlands preservation and promoting trails within the province.

The Stawamus Chief, a massive granitic dome, rises above Squamish—a once-gritty timber community since transformed into a premier trail town. Towering 2,300 feet above the head of Howe Sound, the Stawamus Chief, with its three summits and sheer rock faces, is one of the largest granite monoliths in the world and is coveted by rock climbers. Hikers can ascend the summits via steep and exhilarating trails that use bolted chains and stairways in places. Shannon Falls, British Columbia's third-highest waterfall, is within its shadows. The waters roar and plummet more than 1,000 feet down sheer granite cliffs hemmed by towering conifers. A popular trail leads to their base.

Visible from the Stawamus Chief and dwarfing the valley below is glacier-capped Atwell Peak, part of the Mount Garibaldi mastiff. A massive stratovolcano, 8,786-foot Mount Garibaldi was named for the great Italian patriot Giuseppe Garibaldi. The Squamish people called the mountain "Grimy One" in reference to the Cheekye River's muddy waters flowing down its southwestern flanks.

Hike 9 miles to Panorama Ridge, which overlooks the turquoise waters of Garibaldi Lake, and be overpowered by a sheen of whiteness. The shimmering lake sits at the base of the enormous Garibaldi Neve and other ice fields that feed it through cascading waters. The lake's hue is spellbinding and its origin

Garibaldi Lake and Mount Garibaldi, Garibaldi Provincial Park, British Columbia

mind-blowing. It was formed 9,000 years ago by the Barrier, a nearly 100-foot-thick, 1.2-mile-long lava dam across Rubble Creek. Releasing past debris flows, the Barrier is dangerous and unstable. The trail to Garibaldi Lake skirts away and above it.

Garibaldi Lake, the volcanic mastiff, and the surrounding peaks, glaciers, and deep valleys of ancient forests lie within Garibaldi Provincial Park. The BCMC helped establish this sprawling 481,000-acre park, most of which is remote wilderness. However, within the western reaches of the park near Squamish and Whistler are more than 50 miles of trails. The park's extensive backcountry camping areas make good bases for hiking farther to the enchanting Elfin Lakes, Gargoyles, Mamquam Lake, Helm Lake, Cheakamus Lake, and the Black Tusk—a 7,608-foot volcanic plug. Known to the Squamish people as the "Landing Place of the Thunderbird," the Black Tusk can be summited by scrambling up a heart-racing exposed chimney.

Hikers looking for easier approaches to lofty destinations can secure a gondola from Whistler Village to the top of 7,156-foot Whistler Mountain. Then hike across the Musical Bumps of Piccolo, Oboe, and Flute, enjoying horizon-spanning views that may have you twirling like Julie Andrews. The Sea to Sky Gondola in Squamish will whisk you a half mile up a mountainside to trails leading to sweeping views, including an aerial perspective of the Stawamus Chief. On the return, grab a beer at the gondola station lodge, and then hike the Sea to Sky Trail 5 miles downhill, passing Upper Shannon Falls en route.

Black Tusk and Helm Lake, Garibaldi Provincial Park, British Columbia (left); Stream through Garibaldi Provincial Park, British Columbia (right)

EASTERN WASHINGTON

If you hike up 7,257-foot Mount Bonaparte in the Okanogan Highlands, you may feel like you're in another time zone—not Eastern, Central, or Mountain, but Past. There are old weathered signs, pine-needle-shrouded tread revealing little passage, old gnarled conifers, a 1914 fire lookout cabin on the summit, and views revealing not one hint that the modern world exists below.

The mountains and channeled scablands of Eastern Washington are far removed from the bustling cities of Puget Sound. Trails traversing them offer some of the best opportunities in the state to experience solitude. Eastern Washington's mountain ranges form the transition zone between the coastal Cascades and interior Rockies, resulting in rich biological diversity. Lynx, bighorn sheep, cougars, moose, and wolves flourish in the state's empty northeastern corner.

Black bear, Clackamas Mountain, Okanogan-Wenatchee National Forest, Washington

Along the lofty, lumpy spine of the Kettle River Range, amble on the Kettle Crest Trail (part of the Pacific Northwest Trail) for 44 miles to savor serenity and horizon-spanning scenery. Hike through pine and larch forests and over broad summits carpeted in wildflowers. Pass the oldest fire lookout in the state on Columbia Mountain and sacred Colville tribe vision-questing sites on White Mountain. From Copper Butte, the highest peak in the range, revel in far-reaching views to Idaho, the North Cascades, and British Columbia's Monashee Mountains.

The Thirteenmile Canyon Trail winds 17 miles through some of the most lonely and rugged backcountry in Eastern Washington. Traverse a narrow canyon flanked by towering granite walls, and then hike across golden hillsides, groves of stately old-growth ponderosa pine, and sprawling meadows awash with wildflowers.

Along lonely Crowell Ridge in northeastern Washington's Salmo-Priest Wilderness, roam for 7 miles across alpine meadows and subalpine forest, cherishing views of the rugged Selkirk Mountains and deep Pend Oreille Valley. Saunter through bear-grass flats and groves of trees scratched by copious bears. One of the last bastions in the state for grizzly bears, Crowell Ridge is one of Washington's wildest places. The popular 19-mile Salmo-Priest Loop winds through the most impressive old-growth cedar forest this side of the Cascades. It then darts into Idaho and back, romping along the high, rolling, wildflower-carpeted Shedroof Divide, with its breathtaking views of sprawling Priest Lake far below.

Hovering above Spokane, Washington's second-largest city, is 5,883-foot Mount Spokane, with its elegant CCC-built stone Vista House. The well-rounded Selkirk Mountain, with its thick forest cover and granite outcroppings, looks straight out of the Appalachians. Contained within Washington's largest state park, hikers have more than 100 miles of trails at their feet in its 13,900 acres. Chances are good of seeing a member of the Spokane Mountaineers here. The club, which was founded by five women in 1915, has been instrumental in protecting the park and other wildlands near the city.

The Blue Mountains spill over from Oregon into Washington's southeastern corner. Follow the 16-mile Mount Misery Trail across the rooftop of Washington's Blues into the 177,465-acre Wenaha-Tucannon Wilderness. Traverse lonely mile-high ridges flush with wildflower meadows and groves of larch, pine, and fir, and savor sweeping views of lofty jagged Idaho summits flanking Hells Canyon and Oregon's Wallowa Mountains snagging puffy white clouds.

The Blues are sacred grounds to the Nez Perce. Chief Joseph and his band traveled the Mount Misery Trail to berry patches and hunting and grazing grounds. At Indian Corral, they raced horses. The trail's western end provides access to 6,387-foot Oregon Butte, the highest summit in Washington's Blues. Here admire a historic 1931 fire lookout and sweeping views of tableland ridges above deep forested canyons cut by pristine waterways.

The Columbia Plateau is a sprawling area between the Columbia River and Spokane consisting of ancient basalt flows scoured and shaped by Ice Age floods into channeled scablands. Receiving little precipitation, this land of shrub-steppe canyons, coulees, sand dunes, and mesas possesses incredible geological and biological diversity. Hike up the massive basaltic Steamboat Butte within the Grand Coulee and try to visualize the floods of biblical proportions that carved out the Channeled Scablands before you. As in the past, geological and climatic forces will continue to change the landscape.

View of Kettle Mountains from Kettle Crest Trail section of Pacific Northwest Trail, Colville National Forest, Washington

Exploring Washington *and* Southwestern British Columbia

Trail through blooming
balsamroot and lupine,
Columbia Hills Historical
State Park, Washington

FOLLOWING SPREAD: Columbia
River from Beacon Rock,
Beacon Rock State Park,
Washington (left); Beacon
Rock Trail, Beacon Rock
State Park, Washington
(right, top and bottom)

PREVIOUS SPREAD: Giants Graveyard from Third Beach, Olympic National Park, Washington (top left); Sea lion at Scotts Bluff, Olympic National Park, Washington (bottom left); Quillayute River, Olympic National Park, Washington (right)

OPPOSITE: Rialto Beach, Olympic National Park, Washington

FOLLOWING SPREAD: Sunbeams through Sitka spruce near Yellow Banks, Olympic National Park, Washington (left); Olympic coastline, Olympic National Park, Washington (right)

PREVIOUS SPREAD: Eroded sandstone boulder near Sand Point, Olympic National Park, Washington

LEFT: Point of the Arches, Shi Shi Beach, Olympic National Park, Washington (top and bottom)

OPPOSITE: Shi Shi Beach Trail, Olympic National Park, Washington

FOLLOWING SPREAD: Bridge along Shi Shi Beach Trail, Olympic National Park, Washington (top left); Sand Point Trail, Olympic National Park, Washington (bottom left); Native American petroglyphs along the coast, Olympic National Park, Washington (right)

PREVIOUS SPREAD: Rialto Beach and distant James Island, Olympic National Park, Washington

LEFT: Cape Alava Trail toward Lake Ozette, Olympic National Park, Washington

OPPOSITE: North Fork Skokomish River from Skokomish River Trail, Olympic National Park, Washington

FOLLOWING SPREAD: Marmot Lake, Olympic National Park, Washington (left); Black bear, LaCrosse Basin, Olympic National Park, Washington (top right); Mule deer, Royal Basin, Olympic National Park, Washington (bottom right)

PREVIOUS SPREAD: Clearing storm over Mount Steel from LaCrosse Basin, Olympic National Park, Washington

OPPOSITE: Deer Ridge Trail section of Pacific Northwest Trail, Olympic National Park, Washington

RIGHT: Boulder Creek below Upper Boulder Creek Falls, Olympic National Park, Washington

FOLLOWING SPREAD: Heart Lake, Sol Duc Park, Olympic National Park, Washington (left); Tarn in Seven Lakes Basin, Olympic National Park, Washington (top right); High Divide above Seven Lakes Basin, Olympic National Park, Washington (bottom right)

PREVIOUS SPREAD: Old-growth cedar along Lewis River Trail, Gifford Pinchot National Forest, Washington (left); Lewis River from Lewis River Trail, Gifford Pinchot National Forest, Washington (right)

OPPOSITE: Cedar grove along Lewis River Trail, Gifford Pinchot National Forest, Washington

RIGHT: Falls Creek Falls, Gifford Pinchot National Forest, Washington

FOLLOWING SPREAD: Outlet Falls along Outlet Creek, Gifford Pinchot National Forest, Washington (left); Mount Adams from near Lava Springs, Washington (right)

PREVIOUS SPREAD: Mount St. Helens and eruption impact area, Mount St. Helens National Volcanic Monument, Washington (left); Mount St. Helens from Pacific Crest Trail, Washington (top right); Surprise Lake, Sawtooth Berry Fields, Washington (bottom right)

LEFT: Lava Canyon, Mount St. Helens National Volcanic Monument, Washington

OPPOSITE: Gilbert Peak (left) and Old Snowy (right) from above Lost Lake, Goat Rocks Wilderness, Washington

FOLLOWING SPREAD: Pacific Crest Trail along ridgeline, Goat Rocks Wilderness, Washington (left); Alpine meadow below Bear Creek Mountain, Goat Rocks Wilderness, Washington (top right); Pacific Crest Trail toward Mount Rainier, Goat Rocks Wilderness, Washington (bottom right)

LEFT: Carbon Glacier from above Mystic Lake, Mount Rainier National Park, Washington

OPPOSITE: Mount Rainier and field of lupine along Naches Loop Trail, Mount Rainier National Park, Washington

FOLLOWING SPREAD: Colchuck Lake, Alpine Lakes Wilderness, Washington (left); Little Annapurna over Rune and Talisman Lakes, Enchantment Lakes Basin, Alpine Lakes Wilderness, Washington (right)

Lake Ann Trail, Okanogan-
Wenatchee National Forest,
Washington

FOLLOWING SPREAD: Upper
Tank Lake, Alpine Lakes
Wilderness, Washington

Cathedral Rock and distant Mount Daniel, Alpine Lakes Wilderness, Washington

FOLLOWING SPREAD: Blanca Lake, Henry M. Jackson Wilderness, Washington (left); Second-growth forest along Wallace Falls Trail, Wallace Falls State Park, Washington (top right); Trail through Meander Meadow below Kodak Peak, Henry M. Jackson Wilderness, Washington (bottom right)

Glacier Peak from Red Pass,
Glacier Peak Wilderness,
Washington

FOLLOWING SPREAD: High Pass
Trail toward Glacier Peak,
Glacier Peak Wilderness,
Washington (top left); Lyman
Lake and Chiwawa Mountain,
Glacier Peak Wilderness,
Washington (bottom left);
North Lake, Lake Chelan-
Sawtooth Wilderness,
Washington (right)

PREVIOUS SPREAD: Magic Mountain, North Cascades National Park, Washington (left); Trail through old-growth western red cedar, Big Beaver Valley, North Cascades National Park, Washington (right)

OPPOSITE: Mount Challenger and Whatcom Peak, North Cascades National Park, Washington

FOLLOWING SPREAD: Challenger Glacier, North Cascades National Park, Washington

PREVIOUS SPREAD: Middle Lake, North Cascades National Park, Washington (left); Mount Redoubt from Copper Mountain Trail, North Cascades National Park, Washington (right)

OPPOSITE: Pond below Upper Cathedral Lake, Upper Cathedral Basin, Pasayten Wilderness, Washington

RIGHT: Larch in autumn color from Upper Cathedral Basin, Pasayten Wilderness, Washington (top); Hozomeen Mountain from Freezeout Lake, Pasayten Wilderness, Washington (bottom)

FOLLOWING SPREAD: Forest along Baker River Trail, North Cascades National Park, Washington (left); Mount Baker from Artist Point, Mount Baker Wilderness, Washington (right)

PREVIOUS SPREAD: Ascending Ruth Mountain, North Cascades National Park, Washington (left); Bald eagle along Skagit River, Washington (top right); Marmot, Boston Basin, North Cascades National Park, Washington (bottom right)

OPPOSITE: Nooksack Cirque from Hannegan Peak, North Cascades National Park, Washington

FOLLOWING SPREAD: Pacific Crest Trail from Red Pass, Glacier Peak Wilderness, Washington (left); Deer above White Rock Lakes, Glacier Peak Wilderness, Washington (right)

PREVIOUS SPREAD: Cathedral Peak from Apex Mountain, Pasayten Wilderness, Washington (left); Liberty Bell Mountain from near Washington Pass, Okanogan-Wenatchee National Forest, Washington (right)

OPPOSITE: Marmot, Pasayten Wilderness, Washington

FOLLOWING SPREAD: Pacific Crest Trail near Harts Pass, Pasayten Wilderness, Washington (top left); Pacific Crest Trail toward Rock Pass, Pasayten Wilderness, Washington (bottom left); Pacific Crest Trail along Tamarack Peak, Pasayten Wilderness, Washington (right)

Mount Baker from Gold Run Pass, Mount Baker Wilderness, Washington

FOLLOWING SPREAD: West Coast Trail, Carmanah Walbran Provincial Park, Vancouver Island, British Columbia (left and right)

Coastline along Juan de Fuca Marine Trail, Botanical Beach Provincial Park, Vancouver Island, British Columbia

FOLLOWING SPREAD: Salal on beached log, Juan de Fuca Marine Trail, Botanical Beach Provincial Park, Vancouver Island, British Columbia (left); Juan de Fuca Marine Trail, Botanical Beach Provincial Park, Vancouver Island, British Columbia (right)

PREVIOUS SPREAD: Alpine tarns along Flower Ridge Trail, Strathcona Provincial Park, Vancouver Island, British Columbia (left, top and bottom); Flower Ridge Trail, Strathcona Provincial Park, Vancouver Island, British Columbia (right)

OPPOSITE: Heather Trail ascending Three Brothers Mountain, E. C. Manning Provincial Park, British Columbia

FOLLOWING SPREAD: Sumallo Grove Nature Trail through old-growth cedar and Douglas fir, E. C. Manning Provincial Park, British Columbia (left); Mount Slesse, British Columbia (top right); Black Tusk, Garibaldi Provincial Park, British Columbia (bottom right)

PREVIOUS SPREAD: Dry Falls
cataract, Sun Lakes-Dry Falls
State Park, Washington

OPPOSITE: Umatilla Rock Trail
toward Dry Falls cataract,
Sun Lakes-Dry Falls State
Park, Washington

FOLLOWING SPREAD: Basalt
outcroppings along Goose
Lake Plateau Trail, Columbia
National Wildlife Refuge,
Washington (left); Priest
Rapids Trail and Columbia
River, Priest Rapids Wildlife
Area, Washington (right)

PREVIOUS SPREAD: Ancient Lakes Trail, Ancient Lakes Basin, Quincy Wildlife Recreation Area, Washington (top left); Waterfall below Judith Pools from Ancient Lakes Trail, Quincy Wildlife Recreation Area, Washington (bottom left); Desert lupine along Trail Lake, Trail Lake Coulee, Washington (right)

OPPOSITE: Ancient Lakes Trail toward Ancient Lakes, Washington

FOLLOWING SPREAD: Palouse Falls, Palouse Falls State Park, Washington

Afterword

CRAIG ROMANO

While Pacific Northwest hikers today have thousands of miles of trails to some of the most breathtaking natural environments on the planet at their feet, they cannot be complacent when it comes to their stewardship. Our parks and forests and the trails that traverse them have chronically been underfunded by governing agencies, threatening their integrity and sustainability. Meanwhile, our trails and public lands face substantial increasing use.

Fortunately, countless advocates, activists, and volunteers have worked hard over the years to secure, protect, and enrich our trails and public lands. As trail users, we are indebted to them, and we owe it to the next generation to make sure that these trails and places remain protected and open to all Americans. We have a moral and ethical obligation to give back to the trails and wild places that give us so much pleasure.

Get involved. Organizations like the Washington Trails Association and the Trailkeepers of Oregon have saved, enhanced, and built hundreds of miles of trails. Consider joining and supporting them. They are welcoming, inclusive nonprofit organizations that are vital to maintaining our trail systems. And also consider supporting organizations like Washington's National Park Fund, Friends of the Columbia Gorge, Mazamas, The Mountaineers, Spokane Mountaineers, Pacific Crest Trail Association, Pacific Northwest Trail Association, BC Parks Foundation, BC Mountaineering Club, or Outdoor Club of Victoria. Their various goals include outdoor education and advocacy for the protection of our wild and threatened places.

Fragrance Lake Trail, Larrabee State Park, Washington

First published in the United States of America in 2020 by
Rizzoli International Publications, Inc.
300 Park Avenue South
New York, NY 10010
www.rizzoliusa.com

Trailkeepers of Oregon (TKO) is a nonprofit organization whose mission is to protect and enhance the Oregon hiking experience through advocacy, stewardship, outreach, and education. For more information, please visit trailkeepersoforegon.org.

Washington Trails Association (WTA) is a nonprofit organization that mobilizes hikers and everyone who loves the outdoors to explore, steward, and champion public lands and trails in Washington State. For more information, please visit wta.org.

Publisher: Charles Miers
Associate Publisher: James Muschett
Managing Editor: Lynn Scrabis
Text: Craig Romano and William L. Sullivan
Foreword: Daniel Evans
Editor: Candice Fehrman
Design: Susi Oberhelman
Endpaper Maps: Lisa Holmes/Yulan Studio

Printed in Hong Kong

2020 2021 2022 2023 / 10 9 8 7 6 5 4 3 2 1

ISBN: 978-0-8478-6766-0

Library of Congress Control Number: 2020934268

Visit us online:
Facebook.com/RizzoliNewYork
Twitter: @Rizzoli_Books
Instagram.com/RizzoliBooks
Pinterest.com/RizzoliBooks
Youtube.com/user/RizzoliNY
Issuu.com/Rizzoli

ABOVE: Pacific tree frog, Snake Lake Nature Trail, Tacoma, Washington

PAGE 1: Heather Trail, Three Brothers Mountain, E. C. Manning Provincial Park, British Columbia

PAGES 2-3: Boardwalk section of Sand Point Trail, Olympic National Park, Washington

PAGES 4-5: Mount Challenger from Whatcom Pass, North Cascades National Park, Washington

PAGES 34-35: Temperate forest along Eagle Creek Trail, Columbia Wilderness, Oregon (left); Bear grass, Jefferson Park, Mount Jefferson Wilderness, Oregon (middle left); Deer resting on Pacific Crest Trail, Trinity Alps Wilderness, California (middle right); Wildflower, Panther Creek area, Washington (right)

PAGES 172-173: Raven near Chinook Pass, Mount Rainier National Park, Washington (left); Tree polypore along Snake Lake Nature Trail, Tacoma, Washington (middle left); Marmot, Boston Basin, North Cascades National Park, Washington (middle right); Dew on lupine leaf, Indian Heaven Wilderness, Washington (right)

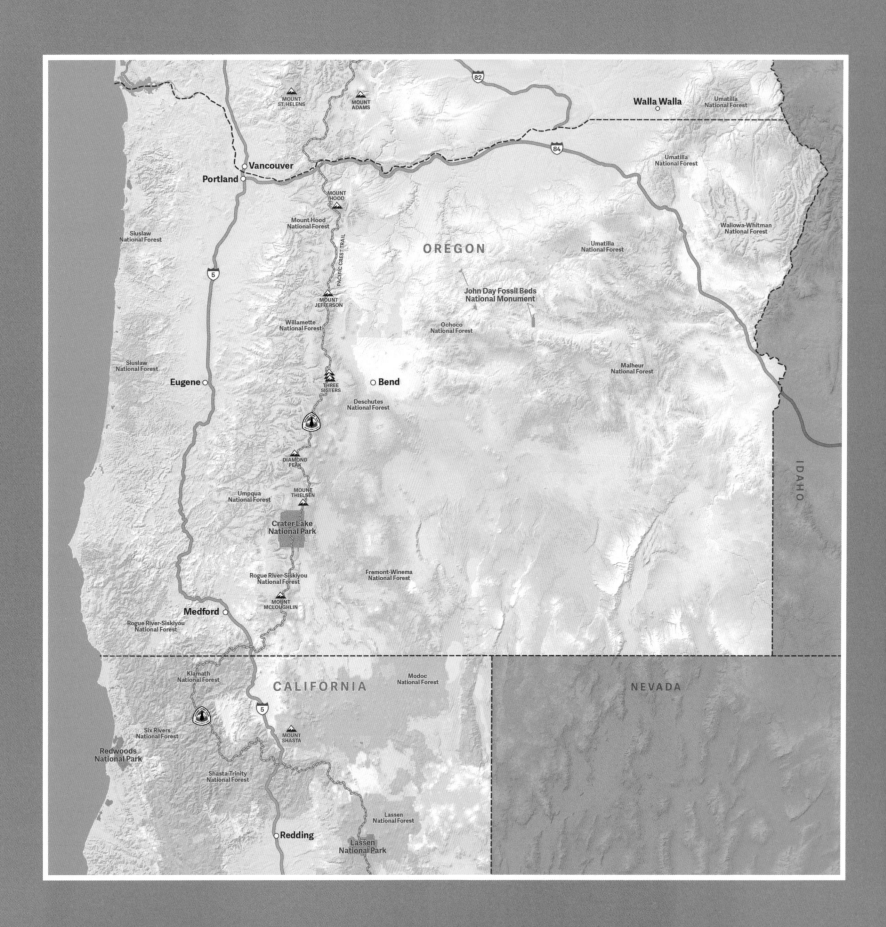